Improvisation

of related interest

Receptive Methods in Music Therapy
Techniques and Clinical Applications for Music Therapy Clinicians, Educators and Students
Denise Grocke and Tony Wigram
ISBN 1 84310 413 X

Songwriting
Methods, Techniques and Clinical Applications for Music Therapy Clinicians, Educators and Students
Edited by Felicity Baker and Tony Wigram
Foreword by Even Ruud
ISBN 1 84310 356 7

A Comprehensive Guide to Music Therapy
Theory, Clinical Practice, Research and Training
Tony Wigram, Inge Nygaard Pedersen and Lars Ole Bonde
ISBN 1 84310 083 5
Free accompanying CD and CD-ROM

Clinical Applications of Music Therapy in Psychiatry
Edited by Tony Wigram and Jos De Backer
Foreword by Jan Peuskens
ISBN 1 85302 733 2

Clinical Applications of Music Therapy in Developmental Disability, Paediatrics and Neurology
Edited by Tony Wigram and Jos De Backer
Foreword by Colwyn Trevarthen
ISBN 1 85302 734 0

Music Therapy in Health and Education
Edited by Margaret Heal and Tony Wigram
Foreword by Anthony Storr
ISBN 1 85302 175 X

Music Therapy in Context
Music, Meaning and Relationship
Mercédès Pavlicevic
Preface by Colwyn Trevarthen
ISBN 1 85302 434 1

Groups in Music
Strategies from Music Therapy
Mercédès Pavlicevic
ISBN 1 84310 081 9

Improvisation
Methods and Techniques for Music Therapy Clinicians, Educators and Students

Tony Wigram

Jessica Kingsley Publishers
London and Philadelphia

Ethical Guideline

The therapeutic methods and techniques defined and described in this book are for use by qualified clinical music therapy practitioners and students in training who have completed or are undertaking recognized clinical training.

First published in the United Kingdom in 2004
by Jessica Kingsley Publishers
116 Pentonville Road
London N1 9JB, UK
and
400 Market Street, Suite 400
Philadelphia, PA 19106, USA

www.jkp.com

Library of Congress Cataloging in Publication Data

Wigram, Tony.
    Improvisation : methods and techniques for music therapy clinicians, educators and students / Tony Wigram ; foreword by Kenneth Bruscia.
        p. cm.
    Includes bibliographical references and index.
    ISBN 1-84310-048-7 (pbk.)
    1. Improvisation (Music)--Instruction and study. 2. Music therapy. I. Title.
    MT68.W66 2004
    781.3'6--dc22

2004004032

British Library Cataloguing in Publication Data
A CIP catalogue record for this book is available from the British Library

ISBN-13: 978 1 84310 048 5
ISBN-10: 1 84310 048 7

Printed and Bound in Great Britain by
Athenaeum Press, Gateshead, Tyne and Wear

Contents

List of Tables

List of Figures

List of CD Examples

Foreword

The time has come that this book be written, and it is fitting that Tony Wigram is its author. Let me explain.

Improvisation was introduced into the fabric of music therapy some forty years ago, not too long after the profession was born in the United States and the United Kingdom. In the 1960s, Paul Nordoff (an American composer) and Clive Robbins (an English special educator) began developing their way of working with variously handicapped children, with Nordoff improvising at the piano, and Robbins working directly with the child. Their first book, *Art of Music as Therapy*, was published in 1965, and after working with hundreds of children in different settings, they began to clarify their model in three subsequent books: *Therapy in Music for Handicapped Children* (1971), *Creative Music Therapy* (1977), and *Music Therapy in Special Education* (1983).

Meanwhile, in England, Juliette Alvin had also been developing her own way of working with handicapped children, using cello as her main instrument, emphasizing the need for the child to improvise 'freely'. Her first book, a general text about music therapy and its various applications, was published in 1975, and three years later, she released her seminal work on improvisation, entitled *Music Therapy for the Autistic Child*.

It was Mary Priestley working in London, who first explored the use of improvisation in psychotherapy with verbal adults. Taking a psychodynamic approach, using piano, violin, percussion instruments, and verbal discussion, Priestley would base the improvisations on whatever concerns the client brought into the session, having them improvise sound portraits of feelings, events, persons, relationships, and so forth, and often accompanying them as they musically worked through the therapeutic issue. Like Alvin, Priestley's first book, *Music Therapy in Action*, came out in 1975, and dealt with various methods of music therapy in addition to improvisation. Her improvisational work, however, was also evolving through work with hundreds of clients, and in 1994, an anthology of her writings was published, entitled *Essays on Analytical Music Therapy*.

So far the history of improvisational therapy has involved experimentation and discovery (which one might call first stage activities), followed by formalization and communication through publication (or second stage activities). This is significant because, since its inception, improvisational music therapy has been practice-based-its clinical strategies and techniques have been developed and tested, not through theory or research, but through actual working with clients musically for an extended period of time. It is also significant that these three models were developed somewhat independently of one another, for different purposes, with different therapeutic styles and values, by completely different kinds of musicians. Thus, improvisational music therapy is at once need-based, pioneer-based, and experience-based. It is a form of music therapy that is by its very nature built upon here-now interactions of unique individuals who have their own perspectives, backgrounds, and values. The implications of this are huge, particularly for the third stage, training.

Given this history of individual approaches, it is not surprising to discover that each pioneer trained their own students in their own ways of working. Nordoff and Robbins set up training centres for teaching Creative Music Therapy, Alvin trained students at Guildhall in her approach of free improvisation as part of a larger programme in general music therapy, and Priestley developed her own training model for Analytical Music Therapy. While this makes perfect sense, it conceals some larger educational dilemmas that would evolve as the music therapy profession began to grow: How can music therapists who have not studied with these pioneers (or their protégés) learn about improvisational therapy? And, when there is the opportunity, which approach should music therapists learn? Should music therapists study all three pioneering approaches to really understand the wide spectrum of improvisational practice? Implicit in a pioneer history is the training of specialists rather than generalists, and along with this, there is a hesitance to accept shared principles upon which all forms of improvisational therapy are built.

By the 1980s, these three models had become widely known, the training programmes had produced a number of protégés, and other new 'pioneers' were developing improvisational approaches of their own. The field had become rich with innovative ideas and unique perspectives, and the complexities and challenges of training generalists in improvisational music therapy were beginning to compound accordingly. The time was ripe for some kind of publication that would organize information about existing approaches. In 1987, the present writer authored *Improvisational Models of Music Therapy*, the first textbook detailing and comparing the diverse approaches to improvisational therapy that had been developed to date. From a training point of view, having such a textbook was quite useful for teaching how the pioneers and other music therapists worked clinically with improvisation. And it allowed for the abstraction of general principles.

What was still missing in the literature, however, was any kind of book that would actually teach therapists, first, how to improvise musically, and then how to use music improvisation clinically. It should also be mentioned that there has been, and continues to be, a lack of agreement on what the instrument of choice should be for the improvisational music therapist. This varies not only according to the model and client population for which it was developed, but also on whether the work is done in an individual or group setting. Should the therapist improvise on the piano (or equivalent harmonic instrument), the therapist's own instrument (Alvin played cello, Priestley played violin), or on simple percussion? And accordingly, on what instruments should all improvisational music therapists be taught to improvise musically and clinically? Obviously, much also depends on what instrument the therapist in training already knows how to play, not to mention differences in their potential for mastering the clinical instrument of choice.

The first entire book devoted to preparing music therapists to improvise clinically was *Healing Heritage: Paul Nordoff Exploring the Tonal Language of Music.* Based on a training course on clinical improvisation offered by Nordoff and Robbins in 1974, this book was not published until 1998. Though rich in musical ideas and improvisational principles, the course and book focused primarily on giving already skilled pianists guidelines for how to clinically improvise at the piano within the Nordoff-Robbins model. In addition to this 1974 approach to training, Nordoff and Robbins also created improvisation exercises for music therapists, and included them in their 1977 book, *Creative Music Therapy.*

It is interesting to note that, to date, these two Nordoff-Robbins writings are the only ones in the literature specifically designed to train improvisational music therapists, and they both are both from the 1970s. Enter the present book by Tony Wigram.

Improvisation: Methods and Techniques for Music Therapy Clinicians, Educators and Students is a landmark publication. It is the first book to extricate improvisation training from specific clinical models of music therapy. It is the first book geared toward musicians who may be beginning pianists. It is the first book that includes improvisation on different instruments. And it is the first book to integrate musical and clinical techniques of improvisation for both individual and group sessions.

What also makes this book very special is the CD that accompanies it. It contains 66 examples altogether, some demonstrating what can be done with the improvisation exercises given in the book, and others demonstrating various musical and clinical techniques discussed. Wigram is the improviser-therapist, assisted in some of the examples by a colleague in the role of client. These are an invaluable accompaniment to the book, as they stimulate the musical ear to hear the myriad possibilities of using each musical element expressively, while also bringing to life musical discussions in the book. Wigram is a master improviser and a superb musician, and it is edifying to hear how fully he explores the expressive potentials of each musical situation at hand.

It is most fitting that Tony Wigram is the author. Tony is a pianist by talent, and an improviser by personality. He studied music therapy with Juliette Alvin, and improvisation with the composer, Alfred Nieman, both of whom taught at the

Guildhall School in London. Thus, Tony's music therapy training was centred on the use of improvisation. It is also significant that Nieman's influence was not limited only to Alvin's students; he also inspired and taught students of Nordoff Robbins, as well as Mary Priestley herself. Thus, Tony's understanding of improvisation, as originally formed by Nieman, is deeply rooted in styles of musical improvisation that were espoused in all three original models of improvisational therapy. One could even say that Tony shares his improvisational heritage with Nordoff, Robbins, Alvin, and Priestley.

Tony is also eminently qualified as a clinician to write this book. He has been working as an improvisational therapist for over two decades, exploring the myriad uses of improvisation in assessment, treatment, and evaluation of various clientele. He has also written extensively about his work, and presented around the world on his approaches to improvisational therapy.

Tony's experience as a teacher of music therapy has also provided him with the insights needed to write such a book. This is not a book that theorizes about improvisation, it is a book that actually teaches someone how to go about the musical task of building one's own improvisatory repertoire of skills, written by someone who knows what the problems are. In the way the exercises and concepts are presented and sequenced, it is clear that Tony has been teaching improvisation for years, and has learned through repeated trial and error what helps students to improvise and what does not.

So far two important points have been made. To repeat the first line of this foreword: 1) The time has come that this book be written, and 2) it is fitting that Tony Wigram is its author. Now there is only one more question that seems important to discuss in introducing this book. To understand the significance of this book requires the reader to understand the significance of improvisation in the therapeutic process.

People go to therapy for myriad reasons, but underlying most, if not all, of them is one basic human dilemma — not having an acceptable alternative to one's way of being in the world. Those who are in therapy because of anxiety or depression have difficulty finding alternative ways of experiencing their lives in a more rewarding way; those who are in therapy because of cognitive or physical impairments have difficulty finding alternative ways of managing these impairments more effectively; those who are in therapy because of a trauma have difficulty finding alternative ways of integrating that trauma into their lives, and so on. Therapy, then, is about the therapist helping the client to identify alternative ways of being in the world, and then selecting the ones that are most beneficial or fulfilling to the client. In short, therapy is about finding, creating, and evaluating alternatives.

When I improvise I begin with what I have given to me – the musical instrument, my body, my energy, my mood, my intentions. And I begin making sounds, then hearing and reacting, varying and adjusting, then reacting again, and trying out something else, continually moving from sound to sound, cluster to cluster, rhythm to rhythm. Once I begin, it seems like the very process carries me forward, not too much different from the way my life has its own way of unfolding. When caught in the moment, I lose my ordinary inhibitions and am swept into the urgency to keep on going. The here-and-now ignores old scripts; its demands are intense and immediate. To continue, I have to abandon old hardware.

I listen to myself, and try to make some sense of what I am doing. What do I inten d? What do I really want this to say? What can I do with what has been given to me? I begin to hear retrospectively what I have done so far, and I wonder if I can make it meaningful in some way. How can I make sense out of what I have already done, and what has happened in the rush of the moment? What sounds do I want to keep, and what sounds do I want to eliminate? What is the theme emerging? Is there an idea or feeling that I am expressing? I catch a sound glimpse of it. Yes, what I am doing hangs together. It expresses something quite unique.

I begin to repeat the theme, and rework it. I keep what worked, and what I liked, and I try to extend or expand it in some way, so that it moves toward some kind of completion or resolution. It occurs to me that what happens serendipitously, and what sounds occur intentionally are all somehow the outcome of what I have done with what was given to me. Like life, I have some choices, but not others. I am limited by what I do, and I am limited by what I cannot or have not done. Yet, all these limitations make me search for whatever freedoms I might have. I keep wondering: what are my alternatives, and which do I choose?

I continue in the process until some kind of closure seems imminent to the idea I have established. It sounds like things have run their course, as if the sounds have plummeted down their own paths, independent of, yet flowing from my own will. The main idea is now spinning out, reaching toward completion. I know now that if I am to continue, I will have to do something else, and take these past sound ideas somewhere else, into a different future. I have to do something different, but what? What can I do next that will somehow be a sequitur to what is past? What freedoms do I have within the limitations I have accepted? Is there anything new I can do?

I strike out in a new direction, and it feels risky. It's not something I have ever done before. These sounds are new to me. The very idea has never flowed from my intention. I have to be sure that I can manage what I do. I am not sure I have the ability, and that distracts me from the task at hand. The sounds I am making are at the very edge of my being, they are at the blade that separates freedom from control. Will I fail, or will I prevail? I discover a way to manage the sound idea, to shape it. I suddenly realize the control that I do have, and with this, comes an urge to play, to take even more risks to extend and express myself. I am beginning to enjoy this now. I find it comforting to know that I can experiment, and find something fulfilling in my discovery. It's even fun.

It occurs to me that these two musical sections that I have forged out of my sheer will to find meaning actually reflect who I am – they sound like how I go about my life. They are parts of me that I have never explored or examined before. They are new motifs of mine that I have chiselled from the already shaped figure that defines my identity. It's a paradox of who I am and who I can be; who I imagine myself to be, and who I intently work toward becoming.

I stop and it hits me. In these simple, few moments of improvising, I have encountered the conditions of being human, the very sound essence of who I am, and at the same time, the myriad possibilities of who I can be. These are the sounds of my life project – to continually seek and create alternatives to what has been given to me, and to what I have done with them so far. Without this project, I will never be fulfilled and my life will never move toward wholeness. Improvisation is the process of continually creating my life anew.

If therapy is about finding preferred alternatives that clients have not been able to discover on their own, then it seems self-evident that therapists have to be personal experts at exploring alternatives, their own as well as their clients'. To teach therapists to improvise, then, is to teach them how to find alternative ways of being in the world; and to teach therapists how to improvise with others is to teach them how to explore and live in the alternatives of others. Improvisation is the very essence of therapy.

Kenneth E. Bruscia, PhD
Professor of Music Therapy
Temple University
Philadelphia, USA

Preface

There is something about improvisation that fascinates some and terrifies others. It can be the most creative experience in the world, and then again the most frustrating and challenging. The art of composition is inextricably linked to improvisation, and the spontaneous creation of music in all societies is centred around cultural styles of improvisation. It has attained some of its most complex expression in the free jazz culture emerging throughout the twentieth century, and the skills of jazz improvisers fascinate and hypnotize their audiences of aficionados. However, it is still considered almost a magical skill by many, a gift granted to the chosen few, while the rest are left with pieces of paper covered in black dots as their 'inspiration'.

This book sets out with the intention of dispelling that particular myth. Musical improvisation, and the ability to participate in it in social situations, has always been the property of all, not just the chosen few. Whether you are creating a multi-layered harmonic, melodic and rhythmic structure on a synthesizer, or just tapping simple rhythms on a wine glass with a teaspoon, the potential to 'join in' with a musical experience through improvising is inborn and present in everyone. This is the 'ignored' musical avenue for many children in schools where the teaching of music still concentrates more exclusively on learning to read music, listen and appreciate. It is, however, a chosen path for many music therapists as a primary method of work, in the belief that the sounds we make can represent us, and that improvised music can provide the framework for an interpersonal relationship between a therapist and client(s).

I have lived and breathed improvisation since before I can remember, and the experiences I have enjoyed stimulate my mind and satisfy my soul. In fact, it was my ability to improvise that led my professor of music at Bristol University to suggest I might gain something from attending a guest lecture at a nearby college by a dynamic and charismatic French woman by the name of Juliette Alvin. This great pioneer of music therapy gave us the rationale and theory for improvisational music therapy, which has become the skilled and specialized application of music as a therapeutic tool in clinical practice in Europe. Subsequently I found it hard to try to explain exactly how I developed my own abilities to improvise, but I realized that in order to teach others, I had to find a way to structure this process systematically, explain it verbally, and then teach it through experiential learning.

Here is the result. Some chapters in this book are aimed at explaining and teaching musical improvisation, often centred on the piano, but with ideas that can be adapted to other instruments. Other chapters start to focus on therapeutic method, and the application of musical techniques within the therapy process. There is a structure, direction and intention to the sequence of chapters and the ideas they contain. But this is not a book to read by the fire, or on a train. You need to be close to music, to musical instruments, to a piano – because, as you read, you need to take the ideas straightaway into a musical experience. The demand for this book arose from participants in many improvisation workshops that I have done, and also from the process of supervising clinical work. Yet it is in the practical situation that developing skills in improvisation really comes alive. Music is a living experience, and the love of music inspired this book. The ideas in it are wide-ranging – but the intention is to explain in a way that empowers readers into music…to improvise!

Acknowledgements

First, I would like to thank my Danish colleagues Inge Nygaard Pedersen and Lars Ole Bonde, Associate Professors at the Institute for Music and Music Therapy at the University of Aalborg in Denmark. If they had not invited me to come to teach and research in Denmark, I would never have had to develop systematic ways to teach improvisation. They have both been an inspiration and a magnificent support to me.

I owe a great debt to my wife Jenny, and sons Robert, Michael and David. They have allowed me to follow my path, always been there with sympathetic support, and have inspired me with their own special musicality. They have contributed more than they realize to the content of this book.

My very grateful thanks go to Katrina Skewes who, when this book was in its first draft, went through it very carefully and in great detail, and provided important and insightful feedback and critique, together with detailed corrections. The re-writing that followed was inspired by her understanding, enthusiasm and generous appreciation.

Many of the examples on the CD involved Vivienne Howarth, a music therapy colleague of many years standing, who willingly (and bravely) was prepared to be the 'client'. Authenticity demanded that she was given only a few instructions, and no lengthy practice takes. The result demonstrates her musicality and adaptability.

I have been inspired by many people over the years I have worked in music therapy, especially by the guiding principles of my early mentors, pioneer of music therapy Professor Juliette Alvin and teacher of improvisation Professor Alfred Nieman.

A special recognition though must go to Professor Kenneth Bruscia, who filled me with an awareness that there are clear methods and techniques in teaching and using improvisation. Much of his thinking and defining, present in his writing and his teaching, underpins the material in this book. We all owe much to him for giving us such a comprehensive frame of understanding.

I want to acknowledge my own musical roots. My parents, teachers and university professors all contributed, because they permitted me to develop my improvisation skills rather than demanding a consistent application to learning how to read and perform music; so did North Mymms Church in Hertfordshire, England, where I spent 15 happy years as a church organist and choirmaster developing a very wide variety of improvisation skills.

I acknowledge gratefully the tolerance of my colleagues at Harper House, and the ever present support of the Director, Dr Barbara Kugler, who gave me space when I needed to focus on this book. I acknowledge also the hard work of my secretary, Jo Ryan, in typing parts of the manuscript, and of my son David for his expert and difficult work in notating many of the musical examples.

Grateful thanks to Lance Andrewes, the sound engineer, for his expert work on the CD, and to Jessica Kingsley and her publishing house, for her confidence and professional support, both with this and other publications.

Finally, I have learned and developed from all my professional colleagues, both in music therapy and in other disciplines, and not least from hundreds of clients I have seen and worked with in therapy, who provided me with the challenge to meet their needs, and without whom the ideas in this book would not have emerged.

CHAPTER 1

Introduction

1.1 Origins

This book is based on many years of teaching improvisational skills to advanced level music therapy students, and even more years of developing and incorporating improvisational techniques using the piano and a variety of other instruments into clinical work with a variety of populations. It is not going to be a book about the theory of improvisation. That subject is very well covered and explored in a variety of different books and articles, both from the field of music and also from the field of music therapy (Bonde, Pederson and Wigram 2001; Bruscia 1987; Jarrett 1997; Milano 1984; Nettl 1974; Nordoff and Robbins 1977; Pavlicevic 1995, 1997; Pressing 1988; Priestley 1994; Robbins and Robbins 1998; Ruud 1998; Schwartz 1998; Wigram, Pedersen and Bonde 2002).

The music therapy literature is full of explanations, well-documented theories and arguments about the development and value of improvisation in clinical work. This book is intended to function as a method book – a tutor, a 'practice' book that gives concrete, practical examples in the text (and on a CD) of how to explore the potential and freedom of musical improvisation, and how to use that freedom both in developing improvisational skills and then applying those skills in therapeutic interventions. Many applicants to undergraduate and post-graduate courses in music therapy at universities and conservatoires all over the world have learnt music from either the classical of rhythmic tradition, playing from pre-composed music, or staying within a narrow style. They have not been encouraged or given a systematic approach to learning how to improvise. When children start to learn to play instruments, particularly the piano, the first priority is almost always to learn to read music. Then one learns to 'interpret' the music, incorporating all the marks of expression that composers write into their scores, and to create feeling and style in one's playing. Finally, teachers demand that students learn the music well enough to play without having to look at the score – 'playing by heart' as it is sometimes quaintly called in the English language, or playing from memory. One is still reproducing another's composition, staying (within the frame of one's own interpretation) true to how you think the composer intended the music to sound. There are two more styles of playing that I found myself exploring as I developed musical skills – playing by ear, and playing 'in the style of…' (pastiche).

Playing (or singing) 'by ear' is a technique that can function at a very simple or very complex level – depending on the degree to which harmonic, melodic and rhythmic structure have been developed and practised. The process involves listening to some music – a solo melody, song with harmony, ostinato rhythm, symphony – and then working out how to 'reproduce' the music on piano, voice or another instrument without ever seeing the music as a notated score. This was certainly my favourite music-making activity when I was a young child, and perhaps the best preparation (I discovered later) for learning to improvise. It was infinitely more fun than the much harder and more laborious task of learning to read the notes.

It is not easy to explain how this skill is acquired. There are, for example, some notable cases of autistic 'savants' with remarkable musical abilities in hearing and accurately reproducing music without ever learning to read a score (or indeed to read words or numbers). This skill is certainly enhanced by the acquisition of musical knowledge, but also appears to be honed by considerable practice, and an ability to hear when the reproduction sounds 'right' and is the most accurate repro-duction of the original. The main reason it helps prepare for the development of improvisation skills is that one becomes quite at home with picking up an instrument and creating music, without relying on the notes in a score. It is most developed in everyday singing, where humming tunes that one picks up is characteristic in every culture, and is nurturing a musical 'ear' by developing the ability to listen and imitate, rather than to read, music.

Playing 'in the style of…' is different from playing by ear. Here, one gains enough experience and practice in a style of music to be able to improvise in that style. The word pastiche is usually applied to this process in composition, where one actually writes music in the style of a composer, and is more typically applied to classical music where part of music education is to learn how to write Bach chorales and fugues, or string quartets 'in the style of' Mozart. Some enthusiastic composers continue to write pastiche music, preferring to reproduce a much loved and under-standable style than to try to develop a new one. In the 1960s and 70s there was a marvellous quiz programme on British television called 'Face the Music', presented by the incomparable Joseph Cooper. A team of three celebrities tested their knowledge of classical music through musical games that included such gems as the 'dummy keyboard' where Cooper played on a keyboard that made no sound, and the team had to try to work out what he was playing by watching his fingers. Pastiche came in the form of the 'hidden melody', where Cooper took a well-known melody and disguised it in the style of more than one composer – sometimes up to four different styles in a prepared example. This 'hidden melody' was pastiche or 'playing in the style of' at its best, and it was fascinating to watch Cooper subtly adapt well-known melodies such as 'It's a Long Way to Tipperary' or 'Auld Lang Syne' into the styles of Debussy, Brahms or Bach.

Improvisation is a much freer and more flexible way of creating music than either playing by ear or playing 'in the style of…'. It can be more simple, but also more complex, as well as essentially original and idiosyncratic. Learning to improvise is as valuable a skill for children learning music as sight reading and learning pieces from memory. As most musical 'educations' do not typically include improvisation, it is also relevant to stress that it is never too late to learn. Therefore the material in this book is specifically designed and presented to build up musical skills usable in improvisation. The ideas start at a very simple level, and develop to more complex models where many different elements of musical technique and therapeutic method are integrated together. These can be valuable for musicians and educators who wish to develop skills in improvising or extemporizing music; however, the main focus of this text is directed towards students and clinical practitioners in music therapy, and offers them a process for how to start, build up and develop from very basic examples to complex and challenging improvisational skills.

An important and interesting perspective on the art of improvisation, with a particular focus on some of the processes involved in teaching this difficult subject, was recently documented by David Schwartz for his Masters thesis at the University of East Anglia (Schwartz 1998). Schwartz explored the whole process of learning improvisation as a student and teaching improvisation as an educator. He defined his perception of improvisation, the process by which one acquires improvisational skills, the framework and milieu and atmosphere one needs to create in order to teach improvisation, and the structure of an improvisation lesson. This thesis provides remarkable insight into how people experience improvisation teaching, as he undertook qualitative interviews with students and teachers of improvisation.

Learning to improvise can probably be one of the most challenging tasks for any musician, even though one might have thought it to be a creative and exciting experience. This is mainly because you are spontaneously creating music which is your own music, and this impromptu composition can attract the same subjective and objective criticism that any composition attracts: 'Too repetitive, too loud, too dull, not a good structure, no nice melodies, poor harmonic modulations, limited, confusing, no direction, etc., etc.'. Anybody who sits down to improvise, especially as a performance for others, is creating music that is essentially drawn from his or her own technical and musical resources, as well as creative impulses. As one of the most significant pioneers in music therapy in Europe during the middle of the twentieth century, Juliette Alvin (1975) once said, 'music is a creation of man – and that is why we can see man in his music'. (Contemporary writing would refer to 'people' rather than only 'men'.)

However, in his consideration of the process, Schwartz captured the defensive-ness and insecurities of somebody embarking on developing their improvisation skills when he talked about the fears of failure and the inner voices that can become a paralysing self-criticism to the person attempting to improvise.

Typical messages of these voices are things such as:

'You're no good at improvisation.'

'You can't do this! You're not free enough.'

'You can't find your inner voice/self.'

'It's not nice to play loudly.'

'This is a waste of time.'

'I'm staying in control.'

'This is selfish!/self-indulgent!'

'OK, enough!'

(Schwartz 1998).

With all this in mind, this book attempts to bring the study and teaching of improvisation into a dimension where it is fun, satisfying, fulfilling, achieving, positive, practical and most of all…possible. The book will try to provide beginner, intermediate and advanced musical techniques and therapeutic methods that can be implemented both as tools for practice and also as tools for use in music making and therapy. I continue to emphasize that improvisation is something that can be developed for purely musical reasons as well as for therapeutic reasons. Although I stand now firmly inside a music therapy profession, my first degree was in music and it was through developing my ability to play by ear, and improvise, that I found myself able to enjoy creating music. This was the skill that led me into music therapy and into teaching improvisation.

Format

Each chapter is structured in a format that can explain, exemplify and recommend. I will explain the method (linked where necessary to theory), demonstrate with examples on the CD and then recommend ideas for practice and development. There are notated examples in the text that can be looked at as examples and also used in a practical and developmental way. The examples on the CD provide some direction or inspiration for practising the ideas and developing skills. The process of developing improvisation skills can be slow or fast and, using this book in a practical way, the best approach is to work backwards as well as forwards! This may sound like strange advice, but the idea is that revising some of the earlier techniques and exercises to integrate them in later and more advanced sections of the book is important in developing a fluent and adaptable style. The tracks on the CD not only provide examples of piano improvisation, but also demonstrate the therapeutic methods when clients are playing percussion (drums, cymbals, djembes) and pitched percussion (xylophones, metallophones, glockenspiels).

1.2 Teaching improvisation skills

Whoever comes to study improvisation, young or old, skilled or unskilled, will undoubtedly feel vulnerable right from the beginning. The reason is that improvising is a process whereby one makes up music, and opens oneself to the subjective and objective criticism of the quality of that music. Therefore, the teacher of improvisation has certain important responsibilities right from the beginning and it will be of great benefit to anybody participating in improvisation classes if these are given high priority.

Improvisation is the development of a range of techniques and methods

Starting from this point of reference reduces the anxieties and vulnerabilities experienced by people when they are told to 'Go on…play how you feel, play the music within you'. This can be a daunting request (or challenge) if some essential tools, techniques, methods and frameworks by which one can best 'play how you feel' are missing. The 'left brain' processes may often come before the 'right brain' in terms of planning and structuring improvised music, and ultimately this will lead more effectively to purely expressive playing. Some argue that it is easier for an 'un-trained' musician to improvise 'how they feel' because they are not 'imprisoned' by a need to work within pre-determined musical form, obeying musical 'rules' common to certain styles, and facing technical expectations by the 'musically trained' part of themselves that block and limit their spontaneity and creativity. Yet I do have a strong conviction that development into expressive playing relies on the building up of a whole range of skills and abilities that can flow 'as if from the fingertips' out of an improviser without them even having to think about it. Therefore the acquisition of skills and technical tricks is not only important but also helps a person believe in learning improvisation as a method.

Every improviser has strengths and weaknesses

In practical terms, this means that whenever I start with a new individual or group who want to learn improvisation, I need to listen to how they play first and take into careful account their own abilities and strengths. I try constantly to reinforce these as well as drawing attention to areas where they have difficulties or weakness. Besides motivation and a creative attitude, improvisation requires a lot of confidence, and it is the building up and development of that confidence in trainee improvisers that is most likely to result in them improving over time. The area in which people have to develop the most is in listening to (and enjoying) the music that they are creating. It is very easy to be dissatisfied, over-ambitious or frustrated and experience some level of powerlessness. Given the right model, being satisfied and enjoying the sounds is the most important experience for someone learning improvisation, and will form the foundation for development.

Beta-blockers aren't necessary!

Improvisation classes require people to play in front of each other – guaranteed to raise anxiety levels and paralyse inexperienced improvisers. This doesn't have to be. Classes can be fun and the great benefit of learning improvisation in a group is that you pick up ideas from each other. Therefore the teacher has a responsibility to create a healthy atmosphere of enthusiasm for development in the group with genuine appreciation of each other's playing and a genuine understanding of expectations and potentials. I strongly believe in drawing out all the positive elements of somebody's attempts at improvising, sometimes encouraging people to reflect positively at the end of an improvised performance, and developing other people's abilities to listen to what is in the music in order to give the person who has been improvising a feeling of importance, confidence and greater awareness of what he or she did. All these elements create a positive atmosphere in improvisation classes without which the classes will definitely fail.

The value of practice

It's not magic! Improvisation doesn't come as a natural gift, except to a few. Even those for whom it appears to be an inborn skill will experience limitations in their potential unless they find a way to develop their talent. Most of us work hard at it, building up our skills and abilities, remembering to take into consideration many different aspects while we're playing and incorporating them as we develop more and more complex processes. So the process of teaching improvisation also requires giving trainees homework, realistic tasks which they can work on (as you will find throughout this book) in order to develop and sustain skills. However, it can be quite soul-destroying and rock confidence if, when practising alone, everything goes wrong and creative juices don't flow! People sit at the piano and struggle to think of something new, struggle to develop a theme, struggle to work out a harmonic frame within which they can improvise. When all that doesn't work, they may give up and say 'OK, I'll play atonal music then I don't have to worry about any of those things'. Then can come even greater disillusionment as the atonal music jangles and rattles away without any particular structure, direction or consistent expression that can be recognized. Recording and then playing back an improvisation can help people analyze strengths and weaknesses, and is particularly helpful when the memory of what occurred during a fairly long improvisation quickly fades. For teaching purposes, the Yamaha Disklaver is a helpful tool. This is a modern version of the old style pianola – where an ordinary acoustic piano has been adapted to include a computer that records the production on a diskette. At the press of a button, the piano plays back exactly what has just been improvised, with notes and pedals being depressed and dymanics precisely reproduced. It is like watching an invisible person playing, and is a completely accurate reproduction of what was recorded.

Practising together helps a lot and is something that I often encourage for people who are learning to improvise. Try to arrange to meet and play together once or twice a week, because when you play together, particularly if given specific tasks that involve two people playing together, you will make much more satisfying development in your improvisation skills.

Getting the balance right between supporting and modelling

The role of the teacher is to help a person learn to be a good improviser. This is not a space where the teacher can demonstrate how good he or she has become! I've learned over the years that while it is necessary at times to play to the students to show them exactly what I am trying to get them to do, the greatest demand on my skill is how (subtly) to encourage their ability to do something without simply playing it for them. I have found this to be most effective by improvising with students and using specific techniques which will be explained later in the book, including frameworking, accompanying and supporting. Often, when I am improvising together with people, I can introduce them to ideas in the music that will inspire them. If they are listening carefully to what I am doing, they will pick up ideas that I am suggesting in my music and use them themselves in their own playing. I can offer them a frame or break up undesirable and rather rigid patterns of playing in order to develop their creativity. This is where a balance is necessary, the balance between supporting and modelling. It is a danger area because students can be very needy for your approval and support and that must be given sensitively, appropriately and with judgement. People need inspiration and examples but they do not need to be overwhelmed (with anxiety) by what are probably more developed and extended skills in their teacher, particularly in this area of learning. A balance needs to be found, and that balance changes as the process of learning develops.

Teaching improvisation is a complicated but an immensely enjoyable and satisfying process. It is like inspiring people to open up their box of 'talents', encouraging them to practise using those talents and then watching them develop into multi-skilled, expressive and creative musical people.

1.3 Learning piano improvisation skills

People who are trained to play the piano

In musical education, children are taught the conventional building blocks of reading, learning from memory and performing music, and it is not typical that they are introduced to improvisation, even when they take instrumental lessons at school or privately. Therefore, a number of people who come to learn improvisation already have some level of competency at the keyboard, and probably training in the basic theory of music. There are a number of sub-categories under the general heading of pianists or keyboard players:

- *Classically trained, basic skills, music bound:* Many people who have studied piano within a traditional, classical framework, have learned how to play pieces from the music, and have some basic abilities in sight-reading. They may never have developed any ability to play by ear, or even learned pieces to play from memory. Consequently the whole idea of sitting at a piano without music in front of them is frightening. They are well able to reproduce, quite frequently in a very musical way, music from written scores, but may not have developed any skills at understanding harmony and transposition in order to play freely.

- *Basic skills, not classically trained – rhythmic or jazz-style pianists.* A number of people come from a different tradition from the classically trained pianist and have accumulated a basic range of rhythmic piano skills in order to play music that isn't complex, often songs where written or figured chords enable them to provide basic accompaniments to the song. Such pianists have developed a technique for accompanying songs in rhythmic group music with a typical 'left-hand octave' and 'right-hand chords' style of playing.

- *Advanced classically trained pianists.* These pianists usually have a very good technique, and a wide range of classical pieces that they can play either from music or from memory. Advanced classical trained pianists have the best grounding for improvisation because they probably explored music that is written in a number of different keys, have some concepts of harmonization and modulation, have particularly expanded and developed their fingering and chordal techniques and are generally fluent on the keyboard. The disadvantage for this group is that they may actually be quite reactive to having to go to a more simple level of creating music when their experience has been playing complex music that they are able to read from scores written by other people. While their ability to play complex music at an advanced level from a score is immensely satisfying, they may have much less fluent and demonstrably 'advanced' skills when there is no music, and they have to construct their own creation.

All three sub-categories may or may not include people who have trained in music theory, sight-reading, harmonization and transposition skills. Where a trainee in improvisation has undertaken a music degree at university, or music study at a music conservatoire or college, they will probably have undertaken study and training, to a greater or lesser level of competency, in all these practical skills, and also in compositional skills. However, these skills are often taught in isolation, and the integration of competencies to the extent that they can be applied in spontaneous improvisation may not have been either a specific objective or the final objective of the musical education. Therefore while people may be able to play very well on the piano they may not understand how to establish their own harmonic and melodic frames.

People who are not trained to play the piano

Included in the groups I have taught over the years have been several people who have undertaken only very limited and basic training on the piano and for whom piano is not their first instrument. It is fascinating to me that in developing improvisation skills people without formal piano training may often fare better in terms of their creativity and spontaneous playing than pianists with a long training in piano technique, who may experience difficulties in 'letting go' of ingrained styles or modalities of playing. They can often approach the piano in a different and freer way, ignoring or setting aside traditional and expected piano technique (finger play), playing with their fists, their feet, their nose or even lying on the keys! While they may be less fluent in using some of the typically classical techniques such as scales, arpeggios, chordal and melody structures, they may be considerably better at free, atonal improvisation, and perhaps even better at listening to themselves when they are playing. They have less preconceived ideas about how good they are supposed to be and may have less negative self-reflection about the quality of their improvisation when they compare it with the quality of their playing if they were performing a piece by Beethoven. Making such a comparison can be a significant disadvantage for trained pianists who may become extremely frustrated with the development of an improvisation if they compare it with a piece they have learned.

Guiding principles for improvisation

I have established some basic principles to guide anyone embarking on the exciting road to develop creative improvisation skills:

- start with a simple idea;
- listen carefully to one's music;
- practise techniques and specific skills;
- master skills one at a time before attempting to combine and integrate a number of skills.

Above all, I believe the most important and vital element for anybody learning improvisation is to listen to what you are doing and enjoy the experience of doing it.

Besides that, it is often necessary to develop an ability to pause, wait or stop completely. Schwartz refers very appropriately to this where he describes 'Marching onward' (Schwartz 1998, p.44), a phrase I particularly like because it describes so well the way creative improvisation can become trapped in repetitive patterns. This is something that applies to pianists, non-pianists and to those developing improvisation on other instruments or with voice where, when they are confident in how they play, they then continue to play without necessarily thinking very hard about what they are doing. Schwartz calls it 'marching onward', and he describes it as the 'Student marches on oblivious to the fact that the music doesn't feel terribly important or connected'. In the same section, he also refers to very structured patterns of playing such as playing in rhythmic patterns of four and eight (typical in Western music and very ingrained in a common meter style), and the 'Standard style' where somebody has certain patterns or structures in their playing that recur whatever they might be representing or expressing in their improvised music.

I would also apply the 'marching onward' phenomenon to someone who has no sense of direction in their improvisation, but is trapped in a 'repetitive musical loop' where they have to keep playing at all costs because stopping (pausing) would perhaps represent a failure of sustaining creativity! I have solutions to these types of problems, which are typical in even the most skilled and developed improvisers. They are techniques called transitions that allow a process of change in the music to take place and they are described in detail later in the book.

Improvisation is spontaneous and can rarely be repeated in the same way. So while it is not composed music, it is created personal and individual music which, as Alvin says, represents various aspects of the person. To be more clear, those 'aspects' of a person can, and do, include a variety of different influences and elements, because the musical production they make on any occasion will contain and include the past and the present:

The past includes:

- the musical culture from which they come;
- the musical skills they have acquired;
- musical taste and preferences;
- influences in the way they have been taught, or learned, music;
- associations to the past, and past life events.

The present includes:

- current musical 'fad' or interest;
- life events that influence them currently;
- mood or emotional state at the time;
- personality state and character as it is currently developed.

All these facets and influences combine to form a musical identity that emerges in improvised music making. Music therapy in Europe is founded on a tradition of improvisation as a means to engage with people, and to build a musical relationship.

The musical identity of the therapist meets and engages the musical identity of the clients, and this calls for highly developed and advanced specialist skills in interacting with clients through this medium (Wigram, De Backer and Van Camp 1999; Wigram and Bonde 2002).

1.4 Improvisation in music therapy: A process

I encourage people who are training in improvisation skills to recognize that it is a process – it can be fast or it can be slow, or the speed can vary as in moving through stages of development. Acquiring a range of simple, musical techniques is the first step in the process that then moves on to incorporating those techniques into therapeutic methods, as well as varying musical parameters that can colour and influence the quality and style of the music. Having incorporated these elements into the created music, and developed a conscious awareness of the potential for either variability or stability in the music, a process develops of integrating and extending improvisation skills.

The ability to use improvisational techniques relies on the acquisition of specific musical skills and the integration of those skills into therapy methods. Within the music therapy literature Bruscia (1987), in his seminal book *Improvisational Models of Music Therapy*, has documented a list of 64 improvisational techniques that are appliable in therapy. He divides them into techniques of empathy, structuring, elicitation, intimacy, procedural, emotional exploration, referential and discussion, and they include both musical and verbal techniques. These are all concerned with therapeutic intention, and I have used many of these techniques, as well as extending and adapting some of them, adding some new ideas, and incorporating them into the methods and teaching techniques in this book. Bruscia talks about 'Clinical Techniques', others talk about musical or therapeutic methods, or musical/therapeutic techniques, models and approaches. For the purpose of consistency and clarity, I refer only to *musical techniques* and *therapeutic methods*, and will define what these terms mean in this text:

Musical technique: refers to a way of playing or singing where the style, modality and elements are described by musical parameters.

Therapeutic method: refers to a way of acting and behaving where the intention, approach, or frame is determined by therapeutic parameters.

After the initial explanation and description of a range of musical techniques and therapeutic methods, the book moves on to more advanced techniques such as extemporizing, frameworking, transitions and thematic improvisation.

Finally, the book addresses how to analyse improvisation, involving the selection of 5-, 10- or 15-minute pieces of improvised music as manageable and understandable sections where the musical structures that occur as well as the direction of the music can be notated, analysed and explained.

The process of developing improvisation skills and applying them is a balance between the cognitive and the creative, fusing together the resources of structure and organisation with flexibility and inspiration. When something isn't working for a person who is attempting to undertake an improvisation, I frequently find myself referring them back to an earlier stage in the process and asking them to start again, taking into consideration variability in dynamic, in tempo or in style. It is inevitable that when attempting to create music, people become stuck. A blocked or stuck position needs to be 'freed up' or overcome, which is not necessarily very easy unless you have incorporated the elements of the process along the way.

1.5 Musical elements – the language of musical expression

Music is often described as a language, a language with syntactic and semantic aspects. For it truly to be a language, there would have to be a much clearer structure of symbols in it that are recognizable. Science-fiction movies, such as 'Close Encounters of the Third Kind', have suggested beautiful scenarios where aliens actually communicate with humans through a melody that at first appears to be a code, but quickly evolves into a melodic and harmonic improvisation. Melody has many of the components of spoken language with its inflexions and its phrasing. However, my premise is that the foundation for meaning in improvised music is usually specific to the person who is creating it, and the empathic level of sharing that goes on is not precise but is nevertheless truthful in reflecting moods, emotions and attitudes.

Skill in varying and balancing musical elements plays a tremendously important role in developing improvisation skills, and the exercises and processes explained and exemplified in this book will refer consistently to the core elements of music: pitch/frequency, tempo/pulse, rhythm, intensity/volume, duration, melody and harmony. The combination of these elements in musical material determines the style and quality of what one hears. The balance of melody against harmony, the use of pulse and phrasing, the structure of the harmonic frame and the influence of harmonic change or modulation colours and enhances music in an aesthetically beautiful dimension, which contrasts with the more 'primitively exciting' elements of tempo and rhythm. The variability and flexibility with which a person who is improvising can employ and integrate all of these elements is what characterizes improvised music, and it is an essential part of any training in improvisation to be constantly aware of the variability or stability of such musical elements. Watching trainees start down the path of creative improvisation, I frequently note that the initial musical production can be quite flat, dynamically. This is because much attention is placed on what notes to play, and melodic and harmonic structures in the music, whether playing on a piano or other instruments. Tempo often remains rather fixed throughout, with equally little variation in meter, intensity, pitch range and typically without the presence of pauses, rubatos, accents, accelerandos or ritardandos. This is not unusual, and in fact it is often noticeable in the music of clients with whom music therapists work. Perhaps we shouldn't be surprised. After all, the process of creating music is hard enough, without simultaneously having to pay attention to adding expression and dynamic.

But the potential of any musical production is that it incorporates enough expression and dynamic, changing either subtly or dramatically, to convert what is initially a combination of frequencies played with different timbres into an expressive and communicative experience. If the improviser takes away some of the elements, reducing the number that can be employed, frequently the result is to enhance the communicative potential. For example, given a drum or tambour, two individuals, or a group, can play around with rhythms, tempo, meter and accents, and put aside harmony and melody. 'Drum talk', used in group improvisation, can be a more exciting and communicative medium of expression than when potentially more complex and expressive instruments such as metallophones, guitars and pianos are the tools of the experience. For this reason, when teaching piano improvisation, the first tasks I give to trainees are to simplify and reduce the potential material, and help a person explore his or her creative potential with very limited musical tools.

1.6 Defining musical improvisation and clinical improvisation

This book is concerned with offering ideas and examples for learning and developing improvisation skills, but also with applying those skills in the clinical field of music therapy. Improvising together with clients, individually or in groups, is where one begins to employ all the techniques, tools, tricks and skills of improvisation in order to meet their needs and engage them at a therapeutic level. Here I am starting to refer to 'clinical improvisation' as opposed to purely 'musical improvisation'. In England in the 1970s there was much discussion about what was meant by the term improvisation and the level at which that 'improvisation' was taking place with a client in terms of musical content and therapeutic intention. In order to clarify and define an emerging terminology in the profession, a small working group[1] was set up to formulate and offer definitions for everyday expressions used in music therapy. The first and major challenge was to define what we mean by improvisation, and the different levels at which this was understood. The first stage was to offer a broad definition of musical improvisation for the purpose of music therapy, and the definition that emerged was:

> Musical improvisation: Any combination of sounds and sounds created within a framework of beginning and ending.

This allowed all sorts of noises to be included and defined as musical improvisation, and strongly underpinned the philosophy of one of the founding pioneers of music therapy in England, Juliette Alvin, who argued that since Stravinsky, dissonant and atonal sounds had become the 'new music', with the consequence of allowing those sounds in free improvisation. We then discussed how a definition of musical improvisation could be adapted to describe the use of it as a technique in clinical work. As part of this working group struggling with defining these (and many other) terms that are used in music therapy, I well recall the arguments that came up as to when a client could be considered to have started improvising. One person suggested that there should be a musical frame of some sort, to separate accidental (or even intentional) noise making from what we would describe as musical and clinical improvisation. Another proposed that the creation of any sound upon a musical instrument of some sort would separate musical from some other form of sound making. Mary Priestley, the pioneer in Analytical Music Therapy, stressed that from the moment a client entered the music therapy room, or space, any sounds they made may be intentional or unintentional forms of music making. She gave an example of a client who leaned back in his chair and started tapping his finger against the side. It seemed that the production of sound could be interpreted as musical and improvisational provided the context was clearly therapeutic. Therefore the definition that emerged was:

> Clinical improvisation: The use of musical improvisation in an environment of trust and support established to meet the needs of clients.

Note

1   Association of Professional Music Therapists (UK) Terminology Group members: Abram, K; Caird, S; Mure, M; O'Leary, C; Wainer, H; Wardle, M; Wigram, T; Williams, A; Zallick, S.

CHAPTER 2

Basic Concepts in Improvisation

2.1 Musical techniques and therapeutic methods

Exciting, stimulating, creative and aesthetically interesting, music can be improvised by anyone, on any instrument or perhaps even just on a chair, a table, glass, on one's own knee or on the door of the bank when you are waiting for it to open! Creating music is a musical process and involves musical technique. Therefore, for anybody reading this book who just wants to explore their creative skills in making up music, we can call this process *musical techniques* or *musical improvisation*. There will be examples and exercises of musical ideas ranging from very simple techniques to more complicated and integrated styles of playing. The chapter on advanced musical techniques introduces extemporizing and frameworking – improvisational methods that can stand alone for purely musical purposes, or be applied in therapeutic contexts with *therapeutic methods*.

For people working in music therapy, these musical techniques are then connected with a range of relevant therapeutic methods. The musical techniques are employed within the framework of different therapeutic methods, and are exemplified in each chapter with different ideas of how to develop improvisation both musically and clinically. When working with clients, one also applies both the musical techniques and the therapeutic methods within a framework which is sometimes, but not always, determined by the creation of 'play rules' or 'givens' (Bruscia 1987). The appropriateness and application of musical techniques, therapeutic method and the use of play rules (either independently or in combination) is decided by the therapist when working with the client. This may have been predetermined, with some prior thinking regarding the client's very specific therapeutic needs, or it may spontaneously, intuitively and quite rapidly occur during the therapy process. Music making is a temporal process, and in the improvisational approach there is an inevitable and ongoing process of evolution over time, whether the music remains consistent, stuck or subject to continuous and rapid change.

2.2 Creative simplicity as a starting point

Every individual who creates improvised music brings his or her own musical techniques and style to the created music. Consequently, the music they create will be influenced by their own technical skill, cultural background and musical preferences (previously described as 'past' and 'present'). In music therapy we try to learn a wide range of musical styles, idioms and techniques in order to meet the idiosyncratic preferences of all of our clients, thereby establishing an effective musical relationship and therapeutic alliance with them. Consequently, there will be many examples in this book of different idioms and styles where the musical techniques are at a simple level, designed to help the musician and therapist to establish a musical relationship that includes a variety of skills and abilities.

To start with improvisation needs, frequently, to be grounded by a simple idea.

Improvisation is most effective and creative where a simple idea is repeated, varied, extended and creatively expanded.

For me, this is an important issue as I have often watched people improvising where they have run from one musical idea to another, frequently changing the music in order to meet an imagined ideal that the music needs continuously to change and develop. Therefore, the techniques that we will work on to begin with are some very basic and simple ideas. These methods are based on developing improvisation skills on a keyboard instrument but can also be adapted to other instruments:

- 1-note, 2-note, 3-note and 4-note improvisations;
- improvising on a single chord;
- improvising with just one hand;
- melody improvisation alone (on pianos or pitched percussion);
- simple rhythmic dialogue.

These are musical exercises rather than therapeutic methods, and are primarily intended to be used for building up and developing the creative skill of an improviser by limiting material or style. However, they can apply in clinical work, especially the concept that working with creative simplicity is a good starting point both for the therapist and for the clients with whom they are working.

Musical techniques will include many other exercises using specific parameters, such as how to establish and lose pulse in the music; how to establish a meter, change a meter, or abandon the structure of meter in the music completely; how to develop a 'recitative' style of playing and then move into a pulse; and how to develop simple harmonic accompaniments from which one can improvise freely. Many of these techniques are extremely useful and applicable in therapy work. Musical technique will also include adding in different dimensions to any of the above techniques by varying volume, tempo, timbre, rhythm, duration and pitch.

2.3 Play rules and 'givens'

Improvising just for the fun of making music and creating a composition doesn't necessarily require any play rules or givens, particularly if one is improvising alone, and there is no need to agree a style or structure with another. Groups of musicians who meet together to improvise, most typically jazz musicians, have probably already established the musical frame and style within which they want to work, using well-known, well-practised musical structures from the wide variety within jazz music. In music therapy, working with clients who are frequently not 'trained' musicians, it is often necessary to establish some structure and predictability in the music with play rules or givens. These play rules can be musical. For example:

Play rule: Let's start very softly, get extremely loud and then go back to being very soft.

They could also be thematic in nature. For example:

Let's think of a place where we feel safe and comfortable and play that feeling and then gradually step outside the door into a dangerous and difficult world. When we start to feel too insecure in our difficult world, let's move back into our nice safe, comfortable space.

Both improvisations might, in the end, have a very similar style but the play rules for one are purely musical whereas the play rules for another are thematic.

Play rules vary tremendously in therapy work from one situation to another and from one client to another. They also vary in terms of the point at which clients are in their own therapeutic process. Most of all, play rules are structured in order to give some sort of sense of meaning and direction to the improvisational experiences that are going on, either at a purely musical level or at the more therapeutic level where musical improvisation is applied in clinical work. They can add a dimension of containment, safety and security to an experience that may well feel both challenging and unsafe for the client(s). The musical techniques and therapy methods that will be explained in the next four chapters can also be understood as having the character of play rules, but I will return to play rules that can be used in structured, semi-structured and freely based improvisation with groups or individuals in Chapter 7.

2.4 Clinical application – the therapy process

This final section of this foundation of basic concepts is primarily directed towards therapists, and concerns the significant factors that influence therapeutic process and clinical improvisation. The application of improvisation in clinical work can be understood as a process that involves different functions. Many have developed a short, memorable acronym to describe a method or concept that represents their theory, and for the process defining the function of improvisation in music therapy I have used perhaps the most obvious word – MUSIC.

Table 2.1 MUSIC – a process

M	Motivation	Why should we go into this experience?
U	Understanding	What does the experience mean for us?
S	Sensitivity	How are we going to experience this together?
I	Integration	In what way can we relate to, and integrate the experience?
C	Containment	What can I put into it – is it safe to enter this experience?

'M' represents Motivation
Here one looks for the motivation for making music together, or individually. Why should we do this? What do we need to do? What does the client expect to get out of this, and is he/she open to the idea of improvising? Do we need at least to formulate a framework and describe play rules in order to create a foundation for playing music together?

'U' stands for Understanding
The therapist's responsibility is to listen to the music of the client, or the shared music, and to understand the implications of what is happening musically, taking into consideration the client's clinical background, problems and needs. At the same time, the therapist works with both concrete and intuited awareness of the client's feelings through understanding body language, verbal and facial expression, and interpreting his or her musical and non-musical behaviours.

'S' indicates Sensitivity
When listening to and playing with clients, it is essential to be sensitive to their style and approach to music making, what their body language says and the timbre, quality and phrasing in their expressive playing. This is the part of the process where the music can be experienced as a form of communication, with contour, form,

dynamic and expressive characteristics, and consideration of how to respond in a sensitive way to what the client is doing musically relies on the listening perspective and skill of the therapist. Sensitivity to the intentionality of the sounds the client is making is based on both knowledge and intuition.

'I' stands for Integration

Integration here refers to the process of connecting the music of the therapist and client, engaging and recognizing separate musical identities, and integrating within a shared musical experience. Mutual timing, direction of music, structure of music and the flexibility or freedom established in the music starts to come into the frame and, overall, one is becoming aware of how the client's specific problems, characteristics and personality are evident in his or her music making and are actively influencing the experience of mutual engagement through music. The improvised music and the therapeutic process integrate and develop.

'C' stands for Containment

The therapist often has to allow herself to be open to all the transferred and projected feelings of a client, and to accept and contain those feelings. The music of the therapist and the therapeutic methods used in improvisation provide a multi-layered and many-roomed container that allows the client a space and context within which he or she can work with a very wide range of feelings and needs. Containing a client is part of the process – which might involve allowing some quite important and unusual experiences to occur.

Finally, a word about silences and 'endings'. The experience of music making, as the definition explains, involves something happening within the framework of beginning and ending and the silences at the beginning and at the end are equally important in order to establish the value of the musical pieces that are being created together. It is not always easy (or relevant) to establish silence before an improvisation begins – and spontaneity in the experience adds to authenticity. However, good attention to the process of ending is critical, and pausing for silence and reflection afterwards is very much a part of the whole process.

2.5 Summary

This combination of musical techniques, therapeutic methods and play rules will be applied in the next chapters, where exercises and examples of improvisational skill building are documented and exemplified. I have attempted to work through these ideas in a logical sequence, building up from simpler ideas to more complex ones. However it is not intended as a hierarchy, but rather a process where the ideas presented earlier need to be incorporated into later methods. In teaching, I have found myself writing out a 'reminder list' of earlier methods and techniques, to ensure that the acquisition of skills does not get lost as the process becomes more complex. What to expect can be summarized briefly as follows:

Chapter 3 looks at basic piano improvisation techniques (many of which are adaptable to other instruments), starting with simple exercises and developing to musical skills that have more relevance in clinical application.

Chapter 4 defines and describes some of the most useful basic therapeutic methods, such as mirroring, matching, reflecting, grounding, dialoguing and accompanying, where the musical techniques are given a therapeutic direction or objective.

Chapter 5 begins to explore more advanced improvisational techniques, both for use in music making generally and for the purpose of therapeutic interventions. Extemporizing and the development of musical frameworks in improvisation are introduced here.

Chapter 6 introduces the use of transitions in improvisational music making, presenting and illustrating different types of transition, and explaining why they are so important in therapy.

Chapter 7 introduces the concept of thematic improvisation, where a small theme or 'leitmotif' containing rhythmic and melodic characteristics is used as a basis for developing an improvisation. Rhythmic and melodic forms of thematic improvisation are exemplified, and the influence of transference and counter-transference is discussed.

Chapter 8 presents some ideas for group improvisation, either using instruments alone or in combination with piano. Some of the author's ideas for 'warm-ups' are described in detail, following which improvisational frameworks are explained, giving a format of elements that can be drawn on to promote group process. Concrete, abstract and emotional themes are introduced here.

Chapter 9 presents two specific models of musical analysis that can be used in music therapy for describing or analysing the music in improvisations. This final chapter is intended to provide just two models that have been developed to look at and document the material that emerges in improvised music making, and identify either musical or therapeutic salience.

CHAPTER 3

Musical Techniques

3.1 Basic piano improvisation techniques

This chapter will present and describe a series of improvisational exercises that I use to promote and develop creative improvisation on the piano. The ideas can be taken and adapted to other instruments. The exercises are just as useful for people who have absolutely no training at all in playing the piano as for people who have studied piano, reached Grade 8 and are playing Beethoven Sonatas. The exercises are illustrated with notated examples in the text, some of which give a 'starting pattern' from which to begin. There will be examples of most of these musical techniques on the CD that comes with the book.

In order to develop our skills of improvising we find out most by listening to what we do. It often sounds very different when you listen to an improvisation that you have recorded compared with what you were aware of when you were actually participating or playing. It is a very good idea when trying out these exercises to record something you do and then listen to the sound you have made.

1-note and 2-note improvisations

The starting point I always take with improvisation is to *limit the material*. I notice a common mistake is the novice improviser's assumption that the more notes used – on a piano, guitar, xylophone or any other instrument – the more exciting and creative will be the improvisation. Actually, this often leads in another direction – into the land of chaos and over-production. My first challenge to any new improviser (or even someone quite experienced) is to be able to improvise creatively using only one tone, as exemplified in Figure 3.1.

Figure 3.1: Example of 1-note improvisation

Figure 3.2: Example of 2-note improvisation

Exercise: Pick one note on the piano – for example E♭ (a black note is easier to use for this exercise) and play it gently without giving any pulse to it at all. At first I suggest playing this note anywhere you like on the piano with differing timbre, accent, sustain and duration, listening closely to the sound. For example, play as deep as possible on the keyboard and then very high. Establish a tempo with your left hand on E♭ below midle C and then start to play a rhythm that matches the tempo with your right hand. Bring it to a conclusion after about two minutes.

CD Example 1: 1-note improvisation

2-note improvisation develops the idea, and it is a good idea to experiment with both tonal intervals (for example 3rds, 4ths, 5ths, 6ths) and also the more dissonant and atonal intervals (2nds and 7ths).

Exercise: Choose two notes and use a play rule of playing them anywhere you like on the piano but only those two notes. Again, it is better to use black notes (for example F# and C#) because it is easier to be accurate when playing faster.

In the musical example given (Figure 3.2) I have tried to illustrate how exciting a 2-note improvisation can actually look. Setting the smallest note value at a demi-semi-quaver on the Sibelius notation system (as with the 1-note improvisation) there are periods of thick texture, even with two notes, when using those two notes all over the keyboard, and also moments of quite thin, sparse texture with pauses (spaces) in the music, indicating a more open texture. The score is meterd in common time, but the tied notes indicate that this is non-pulsed music.

There is an example of how to start this using a 5th/4th interval on the CD.

CD Example 2: 2-note improvisation

3-note improvisations

As soon as more than two notes are used, more complex harmony can be created and the suggestions of melody begin to emerge more strongly. It's a good idea to try this with a number of different combinations. To start with, it's important *not* to use a tonic triad either in the root position, first or second inversion. Instead, use a combination of three notes where either one can create a cadence effect or where the notes will create either dissonant or atonal harmony. Again the play rule here is to play these three notes anywhere on the keyboard in order to build up a creative improvisation with limited material.

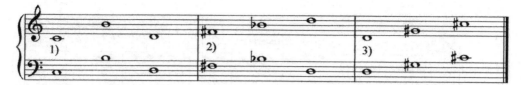

Figure 3.3: Example of not using tonic triads

In the 3-note improvisations it's important to remember not to play all three notes at the same time *all of the time*. Doing so will often create a consistently dissonant or atonal effect throughout and will prevent you from using the inherent harmonies where just two notes followed by two different notes are employed. This is particularly noticeable in the following example (CD3) where a cadence effect of dominant tonic is created.

CD Example 3: 3-note improvisation – cadence effect

In this 3-note improvisation, the cadence created is a perfect cadence where F (C and F) and the use of G (in combination with C) creates a dominant to tonic effect. Using only two notes of the selected three at any one time in the music can establish a sense of key, and cadence. This example also uses the G/F major second to establish some dissonance in the improvisation.

Figure 3.4 shows how these three notes in combination together create a dissonant effect (C#, G#, D). In fact when two alone are played (G# and C#) we have a perfect 5th. However, D in combination with either of these two notes is dissonant. Again, remember to use the notes in combinations of two as well as all three simultaneously.

The next example (Figure 3.5) provides an extremely dissonant/atonal effect of a 3-note improvisation, combining a minor 2nd (E and F) with a minor 7th (F and D#). Bunched together, these notes produce a very dissonant chord but placed apart they produce a more open feeling. It is important to incorporate all the other elements of staccato/legato, soft/loud, etc., to explore fully the improvisational possibilities.

3.2 Pulsed and non-pulsed playing

At this point, before going through any more musical techniques with notated or recorded examples, I want to introduce the very important aspect of pulse and tempo in the improvised music. Pulse plays a very significant and influential part in improvised music making. For a start, it can dominate and obstruct the creative process. Musicians and improvisers who are very 'pulse-bound' are noticeable, because some part of their body, typically a nodding head or a tapping foot, is often emphasizing the

Figure 3.4: Example of 3-note improvisation (dissonant / atonal)

Figure 3.5: 3-note atonal improvisation – E, F, D#

pulse in which they are 'imprisoned'. The result is that the music becomes controlled by the pulse, and by the tempo of the pulse, and sometimes that tempo never changes, nor does the improviser break out of pulsed music.

Conversely, one can also experience playing together with someone where their playing style is so random, uncoordinated or vague that there is a significant absence of pulse, and consequently an absence of any sense of stability in their music. Music therapy pioneers argued that the pulse of music was akin to the pulse of life, and that people with disabilities, affective disorders, illnesses and mental disturbance often had 'lost' a sense of pulse and tempo in their daily life, reflected in their music making (Alvin 1975). Consequently it was the role of the music therapist, through improvisation, either to break up and disturb rigid pulses, or to establish a stable pulse where one did not exist, depending on the needs of the client. However, treat the value of consistent pulse and tempi with a degree of caution as, from a purely musical point of view, the driving force of a stable pulse can also prevent the improviser from stopping to think, pausing, slowing down or speeding up, and allowing there to be flexibility in the music.

In the next exercises, I recommend applying 'pulse...no pulse' as part of the exercise, so as to get into practice right from the beginning at going in and out of pulse in improvised music making. I also recommend working with different speeds of pulse, as well as abandoning pulse completely, in many of the following musical techniques and therapeutic methods to develop flexibility in this aspect of the musical dynamic. An example of a pulsed then non-pulsed music, CD3 uses the atonal and dissonant three notes from Figure 3.5 to demonstrate the need for tempo and pulse flexibility.

CD Example 4: 3-note improv: dissonant/atonal – including pulsed and non-pulsed sections

In later sections of this chapter where chord and melody improvisation is introduced, the non-pulsed 'recitative' style will be the starting point, and further on, in Chapter 6, the ability to make and use transitions will also demonstrate the importance of letting go of potentially rigid tempos and pulses.

4-note improvisations

Choosing four notes to play anywhere on the piano gives one a lot of options, and also allows greater harmonic potential and flexibility. With four specific notes, you can start to build up a harmonic foundation, placing a melody on top (or below) and, with enough variability in style and dynamic, create a complex piece of music.

Exercise: I would suggest using a variety of 4-note clusters, to develop both ton-ally-based, dissonant and atonal harmonic frames. Figure 3.6 gives four distinct and varied 4-note clusters to use for practice. Try an improvisation using each of these in turn, always remembering the following guidelines:

- Make sure there are sections where you just use two or three of the notes.
- Try using these four notes just as chords.
- Try using these four notes for melodic-rhythmic improvisation.
- Try using these notes as an ostinato, with a melodic improvisation above them.
- Try using two notes for a harmonic ground (i.e. C and G as a drone) and improvise melody above them.
- Make sure you play with and without a pulse for periods of time.

Explore the harmonic possibilities in each case, and notice both the logical harmonic modulations (i.e. in Fig.6, Example 4, going from E♭ major to C minor) – relative major to relative minor) and the inharmonic modulations (Fig.6, Example 1, going from D minor or major to E♭ minor or major).

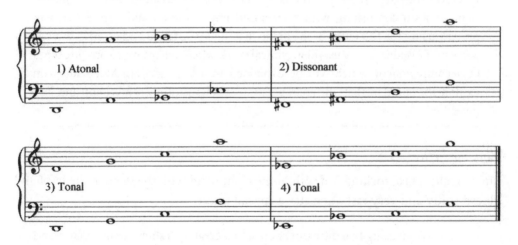

Figure 3.6: 4-note tonal and atonal improvisation examples

This next CD example gives a demonstration of the use of four notes in an improvisa-tion also employing the presence and absence of meter.

CD Example 5: 4-note improvisation with variability of meter.

3.3 Chordal improvisation

Improvising on a favourite chord or key is another good way of limiting the material in order to practise creative improvisation. The effects of keys can be very different: for example it is often commented that A major is a bright, cheerful sound while G♭ major creates a more mellow, soft effect. Consequently, composers have used different keys in their works with this effect in mind, and the bright gay quality of Mozart's A major Piano Concerto K488 is very clear when contrasted, for example, with the Beethoven Piano Sonata 26 in A♭ major. Beethoven used keys in a very special way in his only opera, *Fidelio*, to represent themes such as triumph, despair or freedom in the music. An example of chordal improvisation is demonstrated on CD6, which also introduces what I will call 'shimmer effects' and arpeggio/broken chord effects. They can also be used as accompanying motifs, and will be discussed in 3.10.

CD Example 6: Chord improvisation G♭ major

Exercise: Using this concept, choose different keys to practise creating different feelings. Choose a tonic triad chord – for example G♭ major – and use only these notes in the improvisation. Do not use the scale of the key, just the chord notes wherever they are on the piano (G♭, B♭, D♭). Practise creating rhythmic, pulsed improvisation contrasting with non-pulsed improvisation and ensure that you practise using the full range of the piano in as many different and creative ways as you can. This idea is very useful in clinical work where one wants to provide types of accompaniment which will be explained in a later section. Make sure you explore the chord in all its different positions: root position, 1st inversion and 2nd inversion.

'Shimmer' effect

This is really a fast, rocking 3rd/4th in the right hand with the same in the left hand. Played softly and very fast, it creates a special effect.

Exercise: Try it using two different chords, first creating a shimmer in F major 2nd inversion and then changing to A major 1st inversion, beginning high up in the piano, and then moving down. At first, try this exercise for a short time to avoid cramp. Maintaining a relaxed wrist and fingers will help avoid cramp that comes from overtension. This exercise is notated in the first four bars of figure 3.7. When moving to the A major 1st inversion chord the rocking transfers easily by using the same fingers and changing only two notes in both hands. From bars 5–9, further modulations extend the idea.

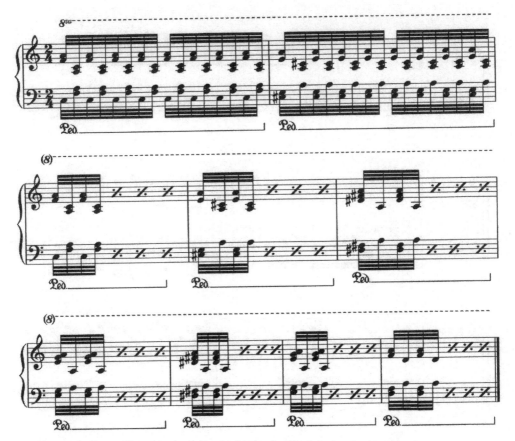

Figure 3.7: Shimmer effect using F major 2nd inversion to A major 1st inversion

CD Example 7 gives a demonstration of the shimmer effect, also using variation in dynamic and, towards the end, the position of the shimmer chords in the register of the piano. The example begins with just F major 2nd inversion going to A major 1st inversion, but then extends to other chords using the same effect.

CD Example 7: Shimmer effect

Arpeggio/broken chord effect

This is altogether less 'painful' than the shimmer effect! Find another chord you like, and explore both with pulsed and with non-pulsed music arpeggios and broken chords. Again, it can be easier to do this on the black keys for greater accuracy at faster speeds.

The example on CD8 uses E♭ minor because it is just black notes and can allow greater accuracy, But it goes on to develop through other keys to give an illustration of how this works.

CD Example 8: Arpeggio solidus broken chord E♭ minor

Figure 3.8: Arpeggio/broken chord effect

3.4 Melodic improvisation – melodic dialogues

This technique is designed to develop the spontaneous creation of melody in improvisation. Good melodies have certain essential components. Quite often they contain some direction to the melody, repeated phrases and even some sense of harmony within the melody. In clinical work, clients present who create melody, but the way they play might represent aspects of their own pathological problem. For example, a client will create a melody which has no sense of direction and which just rambles from one note to another without any sense of phrasing or structure. Another example is a client who jumps from one note to another with no sense of step-wise motion, or who lacks a melodic frame that provides any sense of stability or consistency.

Exercise: To develop skills in melodic improvisation, first of all practise creating a melody that has a simple harmonic idea within a tonal frame, and with some repeated patterns in it. Select a key, such as D minor, and start improvising a simple melodic idea with your right hand. Practise repeating phrases, make sure there is some sense of harmonic direction in the music (for example, going to the dominant and then returning to the tonic) and at first develop a predictable direction in the melody.

Figure 3.9 gives an example of a simple melody improvisation using some predictable and logical melodic sequences, so that the melody demonstrates a sense of direction and coherence. I have excluded any harmony from this, and left the meter rather ambiguous. At this point, I am trying to exemplify the idea of working purely with melodic patterns.

Figure 3.9: Melody improvisation in D minor

Exercise: Left-hand melody. The left hand frequently gets relegated to a very ste-
reotyped role, and improvisational skill using the left hand to make melody is also
valuable. This time don't play in a specific key, but develop an atonal melody in
your left hand. While atonal melodies may feel freer than tonal ones, where there
are some expectations in the implied harmonic structure and direction of the
melody, they can also sound chaotic and directionless, unless some repeated
phrases, figures and patterns are included to give the melody a sense of structure
and coherence (perhaps even occasional predictability). To add variation to the
exercise, try playing alternatively legato and staccato, i.e. in a pulsed, 4/4 rhythm,
do 4 bars legato and 4 bars staccato. Figure 3.10 gives an example of an atonal
melody in the left hand.

Figure 3.10: Atonal melody improvisation – left hand

Melody dialogues

Melody dialogues can be very useful in therapy interaction as they can represent conversational experiences in music. Practising on the piano with both hands can be done
in a specific way where one hand plays while the other hand holds a note, then the
other hand takes over the melody while the first hand holds a note. Hence though the

hands are not playing simultaneously to start with, the music resembles a conversational dialogue between the two hands. Be sure that the phrases do not completely match (by using variation in phrase length) and that some staccato, volume, tempo changes and other variations can creep in.

Figure 3.11 gives an example of melody dialogue, and as a further exercise try using this example as a starting point, extending the improvised dialogue in this style. Note that the melody is rather predictable, tonal, with step-wise and small interval movement, stable rhythm and pulse, and no major dynamic variations.

Figure 3.11: Tonal and modal melody dialogue

CD9 gives a demonstration of a melody dialogue, beginning in F major and then modulating, using melody fragments, extending the ideas and using sequences.

CD Example 9: Tonal melody dialogue improvisation

Initially, it is suitable to develop a melody dialogue without the complications of having to remember key signatures (sharps and flats), so using A minor or C major is a good starting point, if one is aiming for atonal and harmonic idea. The main purpose here is to develop a balanced dialogue between two hands and to develop one's skill at creating matching phrases and answering phrases. Matching phrases can also be played (for variation) in inversion.

Exercise: Practise different types of dialogues on their own at first and then try an improvisation where you mix together the matching phrases, answering phrases and mirroring or inverting phrases between hands. Also remember to vary the phrase lengths in the right hand/left hand dialogue. Start to include accents in the music, and the dialogue will start to sound more like a conversation (as can be heard in CD Example 9).

Melody doubling

An interesting idea, often used in films to create a certain atmosphere, is playing the same melody phrases in both hands simultaneously but four to five octaves apart on the piano. I call this *melody doubling* as the effect is of doubling a melody in another register.

Exercise: Start a simple melody in the left hand in the lower half of the bass section of the piano and play the same melody simultaneously in the right hand high up near the top range of the piano. Try it slowly and softly at first, gradually introducing dynamic, rhythm and tempo to the improvisation. Keep it simple to begin with, and then develop the complexity of the melody when you feel confident that you can play the same thing simultaneously with both hands. An illustration is given in Figure 3.12.

The example on the CD (CD10) gives a demonstration of the type of effect that can be achieved with melody doubling. When playing with both hands far apart, slow, step-wise (perhaps chromatic) music with occasional short pauses is a good way to begin in order to achieve accuracy in melody doubling.

CD Example 10: Melody 4–5 octaves apart

Figure 3.12: 4–5 octave apart melody – special effect

3.5 Chord and melody improvisation

This technique is based on a combination of chords in one hand and melody in the other, which so typically provides a musical frame for songs or pieces. To establish a simple and straightforward foundation begin with a two-chord improvisation in the left hand. Use a 'recitative' style in order to avoid getting stuck in a pulse. The objective here is to establish a two-chord frame (in either the left hand or the right hand), with an improvised melody in the opposite hand without a pulse, where the development of a melody within a tonal frame is practised.

Exercise: Figure 3.13 provides a sequence of tonal chords which lead through a logical modulatory sequence. For this exercise use the first two chords only, at first, to provide the harmonic ground for the chord and melody improvisation. Take these first two chords and work out a diatonic improvisation on the white keys of the piano alone (as demonstrated in Figure 3.13) improvising a melody above the chords. When using the 'recitative' style of improvising, the trick is to make sure that when you change the chord the harmony of the melody logically falls on the right note at the point of change.

Adding meter and pulse

In the example given (Figure 3.13 and CD11), after a period of recitative, the material develops into a meter, with a slow, stable pulse (bar 8). It is still important to remember that as soon as a pulse is introduced, especially when it is framed with a common time meter, the improvisation should initially stay legato and very moderato in character, in order that the improviser has time to think and modify the improvisation as it continues.

Exercise: At first, practise the recitative style illustrated on the CD and in the music. Subsequently, establishing a simple 4-4 pulse on the chords and then improvising the melody to those chords is a good way to develop the idea within tempo. Subsequently (CD 11), switching the chords to the right hand while the left hand has to produce the melody is a good challenge for your right brain/left brain flexibility!

CD Example 11: Two chord improvisation – recitative (chords in right hand then in left hand)

3.6 Dissonant improvisation

Dissonance is described generally as a discordant combination of sounds, and musically is a style that is founded in tonality, but includes certain intervals (seconds, sevenths, diminished and augmented intervals) that give the chords and harmony a dissonant quality. *Dissonant music* is also characterized by incongruence or discrepancy in the musical harmony (Collins English Dictionary 1993). In order clarify differences at this stage, *atonal music* is defined as music that has no established key, whereas *dissonant music* has a sense of key, and a harmonic framework. *Tonal music* is music that is defined as having or relating to tone: utilizing the diatonic system and having an established key.

In clinical music therapy, it is often relevant and empathic to create a dissonant frame to a client's music to reflect certain aspects of the feelings that might be under-pinning or underlying the expressive communication within the music. Harmonically tonal music may not be effective empathically with the client's disturbed or upset feelings and dissonance can serve a very useful function in the same way as atonal music can break free of any types of harmonic or structured rules. Dissonance is useful where a client is perhaps playing random melodic material either on a piano, xylophone or another type of melodic instrument, and the therapist can create a dissonant harmonic frame for the client's music.

Figure 3.13: Two-chord improvisation (F7 to G7) Recitative leading to meter, continued on next page

Figure 3.13: Two-chord improvisation (F7 to G7) Recitative leading to meter, continued

Figure 14 offers a technique for practising this using the piano. The left hand can give a dissonant harmonic frame that is basically grounded in C major with the augmented fourth included in the chord. Melody can then be improvised above it in a different key, such as E major or D major. This juxtaposition of one key upon another is an effective way to achieve a dissonant effect within a conventional harmonic frame. A fine example to practise is playing a song or a piece using one key for the accompaniment and another key for the melody.

Exercise: Practise playing 'Twinkle, Twinkle Little Star' in C major harmony on the left hand, while playing the tune in C sharp major on right hand! Once you have mastered how it goes, try placing the melody two octaves higher than the harmony!

Figure 3.14: Dissonant harmonic-melodic music

This isn't just for fun, as it creates an interesting dynamic, especially when working with children who can be amused and intrigued by hearing tunes that are distorted by employing dissonance in this way. So the easiest way to develop a dissonant style of playing is by taking a harmonic frame and then adding dissonant intervals into the harmonic frame such as seconds, sevenths and augmented fourths.

3.7 Atonal melodic dialogue improvisation

As I described earlier, atonal improvisation is where no particular key is specified and the music appears to be totally ungrounded harmonically. There still needs to be some stability in the melodic style, with repeated ideas, motifs, phrases and rhythmic patterns. Atonal music can be experienced as a chaotic and even frightening medium by some, while others find it a free and creative style of play. This is essentially its value as a therapeutic tool, offering an opportunity for musical participation to all where musical skill and knowledge is not a prerequisite, and where the musical relationship can be an equal-term relationship. It offers the opportunity to explore and balance structure and freedom in music therapy treatment, which has been a theme of mine in previous articles (Wigram 1995b, 2002a).

A simple way of beginning an atonal style of improvisation is through melodic dialogue, only this time play with your right hand on the black notes and your left hand on the white notes. Playing with the hands in juxtaposition increases the atonal feel to the music, and develops a feeling of the melodies intertwining with each other. When the hands are further apart, one's sense of harmonic structure in the musical brain tends to start separating out the tonal and atonal effects, and it sounds more dissonant than atonal.

Exercise: To start an atonal melody dialogue, begin playing melody phrases with the left hand on the white notes, and then pause with the left hand while the right hand joins in on the black notes. Use plenty of seconds and sevenths in the melodic idea to accentuate the idea of atonal music. After two or three exchanges of phrases, practise in juxtaposition, and then play with both hands simultaneously to develop the dialogue into a duet.

The example on the CD (CD12) demonstrates the idea, illustrating the closeness and intertwined effect of right hand-left hand interaction in this dialogue leading to a duet.

CD Example 12: Atonal melody dialogue

Figure 3.15: Atonal melody dialogue improvisation

3.8 Playing in 6ths and 3rds, tonic triads, 1st and 2nd inversions

Tonal structure can be very supportive, grounding, stabilizing and structuring in improvisation. Simple techniques that are easily mastered but produce quite a complex effect are valuable tools in therapy. This section explains how to apply a technique

Figure 3.15: Atonal melody dialogue improvisation

where the position and distance between fingers in the right hand using thumb and fifth finger for sixths, and thumb and third finger for fourths is 'fixed', and attention can be given to phrasing, melodic direction and musical dialogue.

6ths and 3rds

The first technique to develop, using the piano, for giving a tonal melodic accompaniment or support to a client's music is the use of 6ths or 3rds on the piano. It is a simple, harmonic and also melodic way to provide a supportive framework to a client improvising on percussion or instruments or xylophones and metallophones.

Exercise: Establish a tonal centre or a tonal ground in the bass of the piano, using a repetitive pattern of three octaves. For a ground in the major (again using just the white notes of the piano) C-F-G...C-F-G in slow octaves provides the harmonic ground. For the relative minor, use A-D-E...A-D-E.

In the right hand start to play using just the interval of the 6th, solely on the white notes and using a step-wise direction in the melody line, to create a melodic and harmonic effect. It's useful if the moment when the octave changes in the left hand matches in a harmonically (modulatory) congruent way with the 'melody' that is being improvised using 6ths in the right hand. Develop this further using 3rds in the right hand, and by extending the left hand octave improvisation beyond a tonic, dominant subdominant sequence. Figure 3.16 gives an illustration of this technique, bringing in triplet rhythms in the melody which, together with the effects of 6ths and 3rds, gives a gentle, Mexican/Latin American feel to the music.

CD Example 13 gives a demonstration of moving in 6ths and 3rds, using an octave ground bass. This is also an example of the use of rubato in music, where the effect of slowing and stretching the music perhaps provides a wistful, sentimental effect. It is another example of the importance of including other musical elements and aspects when employing a specific musical technique.

CD Example 13: 6ths and 3rds improvisation

Tonic triads, 1st and 2nd inversions

The technique of 6ths and 3rds described above can be developed using triad chords in different inversions.

Figure 3.16: 6ths and 3rds improvisation with tonal bass

Exercise: Use the same bass idea of three octaves, tonic, dominant, sub-dominant (C-G-F), and the relative minor using A-D-E. This time, instead of playing just the sixth, add the third in to form the 6/3, or 1st inversion chord in your right hand.

 When this has become confident, extend this idea by forming your hand into the position of the 6/4, or 2nd inversion chord. Each time, play using a step-wise movement, with a slightly stronger pressure in your little finger to accentuate a melody. Finally, try using the whole tonic triad chord plus the octave. Practise an improvisation using these chords. It's very good for accompanying and supporting playing where a client is randomly playing melodies on a xylophone or another piano. These three options (1st inversion, 2nd inversion and tonic triad plus octave are exemplified in Figure 3.17, and the CD Example 14.

CD Example 14: 1st inversion, 2nd inversion and tonic triad plus octave chordal improvisation with relative major to relative minor tonal ground

3.9 Playing in and out of meter

Having written earlier about the significant effect of pulse and tempo on improvised music, I would also like to explain the relevance and power of meter. Not only do we find the need to ground our improvised music in a stable pulse, with or without changes in tempo, but meter is often present in the rhythm and tempo of the music. Meter can act as a valuable 'anchor' in defining the structure of the music, but it can also function as a musical 'prison', where the presence of strong beats confirmed by regular accentuation establishes a fixed pattern.

The common meters, such as 4/4, 3/4, 2/4, provide clear accents in the music. Compound time, with meters such as 6/8, 9/8 or 6/4 offer different possibilities for strong beats, and irregular meters, such as 5/4 or 7/8, give us a sense of structure with either a syncopated or cross rhythmic effect. Another of the values of providing an established meter is that it allows the development of syncopated playing with unexpected and irregular accents.

Figure 3.18 shows the different meters, and goes on to introduce a chordal improvisation that develops into using 6ths, 1st and 2nd inversions. The example shows the changing meters in the musical material, interspersed with sections that sustain the pulse, but have abandoned the meter. This illustrates how flexible rhythmic music can be, especially when one also remembers to incorporate rubato, accelerandos and ritardandos.

Figure 3.17: 1st inversion, 2nd inversion and tonic triad plus octave chordal improvisation with relative major to relative minor tonal ground

Figure 3.18: Meter, lack of meter, in chords, 6ths and inverted chord improvisations

3.10 Accompanying techniques

Accompanying techniques are very useful in therapy and quite often involve providing some type of chordal harmonic framework to what a client may be doing. This is building on the previous section of two-chord with extended modulations (cycle of fifths) improvisations, and is where one starts to use style to vary the accompaniment in order to support or influence a melodic or rhythmic production in a client's music. Accompanying is a musical technique and also a therapeutic method, so I will introduce it in this chapter as a technique, and then refer to it again in the next chapter for its value in therapy.

Simple accompaniment examples using a two-chord harmony are demonstrated in Figure 3.19, which shows how this simple frame can develop through different accompanying styles. The examples of accompanying using the two chords are made by varying texture, rhythmic patterns, meter and style. The left hand tends to provide a grounding 'dominant/tonic' octave or note, while the right hand varies in style. To begin with, the right hand plays the two chords in crotchets (1), quavers (2), followed by Latin American rhythmic patterns (3) and (4). Arpeggios (5) and off-beat chords (6) are followed by a change of meter to 6/8 (7) and (8). Returning to common time with syncopation is introduced by accents (9) and rests in the music (10), and the examples finish with simple broken chords (11).

Exercise: Imagine a client is playing randomly on a metallophone using one beater to create some melodic phrases and it is the therapist's decision to try to support this with an accompaniment.

These techniques are also demonstrated on the CD (CD15), which illustrates how this can work in practice and the way in which the accompanist begins with a recitative style, followed by establishing some rhythmic ground and then developing a rhythmic figure to support the accompaniment.

CD Example 15: Piano accompanying a metallophone

Percussion instruments are also very good for providing accompaniment and, to move away from the piano for a moment, CD16 gives an example of the usefulness of the drum (played with hands) in providing a supportive accompaniment to someone playing on a xylophone.

CD Example 16: Drum accompanying a xylophone

Figure 3.19: Two-chord accompanying in different patterns and styles, continued on next page

Figure 3.19: Two-chord accompanying in different patterns and styles, continued

3.11 Summary and conclusion

These are a selection of useful techniques with which to begin practising in order to create building blocks for the therapeutic methods that follow. Creativity and flexibility are the primary objectives, and are important factors in developing improvisation that will become musically interesting and therapeutically effective. The most common problem in improvisation is that people find themselves getting stuck in a particular idea and forget all the potential musical variables that can be introduced and deployed to develop the creativity of the improvisation, particularly changes in tempo and changes in volume. Therefore in all the above exercises it is essential to introduce variability of the musical elements in order to add colour, expressivity and meaning to the concrete technique as it is being developed.

CHAPTER 4

Basic Therapeutic Methods and Skills

There are many different therapeutic methods that are applied in music therapy when using improvisation. Bruscia (1987, p.533) began with a description of 64 'clinical techniques' and with the increasing volume of published literature on music therapy over the last 12 years, further techniques and methods used in therapy have been reported (Codding 2000, 2002; Pedersen 2002; Staum 2000; Wigram and Bonde 2002; Wigram and De Backer 1999a, 1999b; Wigram, Pedersen and Bonde 2002).

Therapy methods can either be used intentionally (or intuitively) in therapy work with clients or they can be the objects of analysis when reflecting on a period of free-flowing improvisation to explore what was actually happening. It is not usual for music therapists to pre-plan exactly the method they might use, unless they are working in an activity-based model, or with a structured assessment procedure. In improvisational music therapy, particularly, the model requires an adaptive and flexible response to the way the client begins to make music. There can be a certain degree of planning based on the assessment that has taken place and an estimation of the client's needs and the objectives of therapy that will promote certain techniques above others. However, it is more typical that improvisational music making occurs, and within that music making intuitive judgements about therapeutic method are made based on the 'here and now' experience. Music therapists don't remain exclusively attached to one musical technique or therapeutic method for a set period of time, and might fluctuate between a number of different methods (as well as musical techniques) over the course of a single improvisation.

This chapter presents, discusses and exemplifies certain specific methods that are commonly used in music therapy, in order to provide methods within which the musical techniques that have been described in the previous chapter can be applied.

It is very useful to practise these techniques together with another person, first of all playing the experience and subsequently responding to the musical production of another. Each technique will include a musical illustration, complemented by an example on the CD.

4.1 Mirroring, imitating and copying

Mirroring and *imitating* are frequently used as empathic techniques where the music therapist intends to give a message to the client that they are meeting them exactly at their level and attempting to achieve synchronicity with the client. Bruscia has described the technique of mirroring as 'synchronising – doing what the client is doing at the same time'. I define mirroring in a similar way but with a slightly broader explanation, in order to suggest to clinical practice that mirroring involves more than just musical behaviour:

> *Mirroring: Doing exactly what the client is doing musically, expressively and through body language at the same time as the client is doing it. The client will then see his or her own behaviour in the therapist's behaviour.*

This can only be achieved musically, where the client's music is both simple enough and predictable enough for the therapist to anticipate how to mirror exactly what the client is doing. This also applies to the physical behaviour of the client. In order for the mirror to be exact, the therapist may also need to pay attention to using a very similar instrument as the client in order to achieve a mirrored response. However, it is possible to accomplish mirroring by using a different instrument. Example 17 on the CD gives an illustration where the therapist can use the piano almost as a drum while the client plays on a drum.

CD17: Mirroring – client on drum + therapist on piano

'Close enough' mirroring is a technique where the therapist is doing almost exactly the same as the client but due to technical reasons cannot copy exactly. For example, this would work very well where the client is randomly playing notes on a metallophone and the therapist mirrors that by playing as near an imitation as possible at the same time, achieving the direction of the melody and the general contour of the melody without necessarily matching exact notes.

Conceptually, we can see the identities of the participants in mirroring (client and therapist) in a very symbiotic relationship, where they become fused and undivided. Figure 4.1 illustrates the place of the therapist and client inside two circles where the integration of one circle into another represents the closeness of the material.

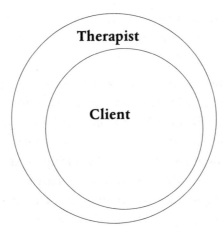

Figure 4.1: Musical closeness in mirroring

Imitating or copying are also empathic methods of improvisation and imitating has been defined by Bruscia as 'echoing or reproducing a client's response after the response has been completed'. This relies on the client leaving spaces in the music for the therapist to imitate what he or she is doing. It should be used quite specifically, and caution needs to be exercised as imitating or copying a client's production might appear as though you were either teasing or patronizing the client. While mirroring and copying are relatively simple methods, they can also be quite confronting to a client, and can be risks, for example, with clients with paranoia or thought disorder for whom this method may excite irrational fears. This approach needs to be used sensitively and appropriately. Nevertheless, it is a therapeutic strategy to help a client to be aware that musically you are echoing and confirming what they have done.

4.2 Matching

I regard *matching* is one of the most valuable of all the improvisational methods that can be applied in therapy. It is, in my approach, a typical starting point to work together with the client musically, from which a number of other therapeutic strategies or methods emerge. It is also an empathic method, as the music produced by the therapist in response to the client confirms and validates their playing and their emotional expression.

I have defined the term to be quite inclusive:

Matching: Improvising music that is compatible, matches or fits in with the client's style of
playing while maintaining the same tempo, dynamic, texture, quality and complexity of
other musical elements (Wigram 1999a).

To achieve a 'match' in musical terms means that the therapist's music is not identical
to the client's, but is the same in style and quality. Therefore the client experiences
that the therapist's music 'fits together and matches' his or her own production.

Conceptually, we can begin to see the two separate identities of the participants
(client and therapist) in their musical relationship, where they are together,
congruent and matched musically, but with some individual differences that show
emerging separateness. Figure 4.2 shows two circles separating, representing the
matched material but separating identities of the therapist and client.

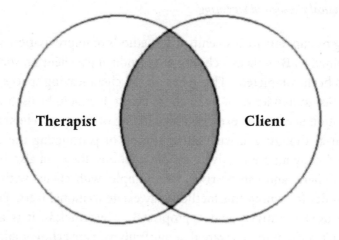

Figure 4.2: Musical connections in matching

Bruscia does not include matching as a term, but incorporates the idea into a definition of reflecting. Pavlicevic (1997) has referred to it in her book *Music Therapy in
Context* giving a different conceptual understanding. She thinks of matching as
'partial mirroring where, for example, the client plays a definite and predictable
musical pattern, and the therapist mirrors some, but not all, of the rhythmic components' (p.126).

My experience and use of matching in therapy is more as an equal, complemen-
tary style of playing together, as illustrated in Figures 4.3, 4.4 and 4.5, and demonstrated in CD18, CD19 and CD20. The CD examples start with the 'client' playing,
and show how the therapist joins in, matching the music of the client. In the first
examples (Figure 4.3 and CD18) the rhythmic style of the client is revealed as short,
quite stable rhythmic patterns in a regular pulse. As the improvisation develops, the

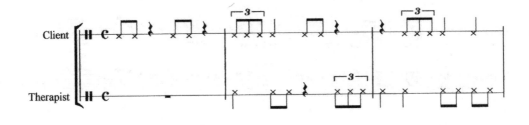

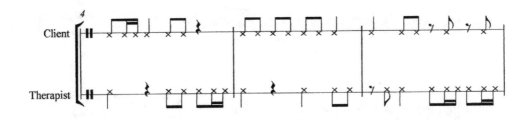

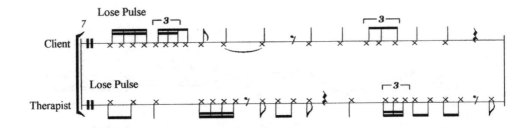

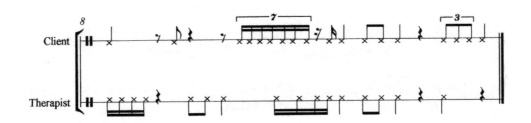

Figure 4.3: Matching: client on bongos, therapist on conga

Figure 4.4: Matching: client on xylophone, therapist on metallophone

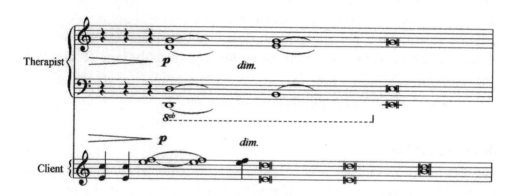

Figure 4.5: Matching – client on metallophone, therapist on piano

style changes with a loss of any sense of pulse in the client's playing, and the therapist can be heard to adapt and sustain matching.

CD Example 18: Matching – client on bongos, therapist on djembe

In the next examples (Figure 4.4 and CD19) melodic matching is illustrated. Here the emphasis is on style of the melody, in particular phrase lengths, step-wise or large interval movement and tonality. The client's material changes as the example goes on, and the therapist can also be heard to adapt to this change.

CD Example 19: Matching – client and therapist on melodic instruments

Finally, Figure 4.5, CD 20 gives an example where the therapist (piano) uses chords to match with a client (metallophone) who is playing sustained, two-tone sounds, without any sense of rhythmic or harmonic direction. In the therapeutic process of matching it is very important to stay true to the client's music, and not attempt to modify, change or manipulate. At this stage of therapeutic intervention, using the matching method, therapeutic directions or 'solutions' are not the primary objective, and may emerge later. The engagement, close to the tradition and goal of client centred therapy, is to offer 'unconditional positive regard' in the form of acceptance and matching.

CD Example 20: Client on xylophone, therapist on piano

Matching exercises

The CD has two examples of a person playing that provide an opportunity to practise the therapeutic method of matching. The first part of the process in matching is to listen to and analyse the musical components of a client's production, also taking into account their level of expression in their body and their face. However, as these examples are presented on CD, the latter information is not available and one needs solely to consider the musical elements.

Table 4.1 identifies the musical elements for these two examples in order to clarify the type of music the therapist should produce to match and empathize with the client's material.

Table 4.1 Structured matching exercises

Example	Style	Rhythm	Dynamic	Tonality
1 (CD21)	Folk	4/4 regular	Soft and slow	Pentatonic
2 (CD22)	Jazzy	Irregular	Wide range	Atonal

4.3 Empathic improvisation and reflecting

Mirroring, copying and *matching* involve a more technical exercise of creating a musically congruent response to the client, attending primarily to the balance and salience of musical elements, as well as body language and expression. *Empathic improvisation* and *reflecting* require a response that is more specifically connected to the emotional state of the client.

Empathic improvisation

This is difficult to illustrate in a book or on a CD. It involves a therapeutic method that was first applied by Juliette Alvin where, typically at the beginning of a session, she would play (on her cello) an improvisation that empathically complemented the client's 'way of being'. In practice this means taking into account the client's body posture, facial expression, attitude on this particular day and previous knowledge of their personality and characteristics, and playing something to them that reflects a musical interpretation of their own way of being at that moment. It was intended by Alvin as a very empathic technique, not attempting in any way to change the client's feelings or behaviour, but simply to play them to the client without any hidden manipulation of their feelings. If a client comes into the therapy room agitated and upset, this mood can easily be incorporated into an empathic improvisation; the therapist is not trying to ameliorate or reduce the degree of distress which the client is currently experiencing but merely to play it back to them as a supportive and empathic confirmation.

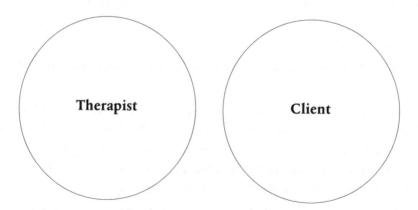

Figure 4.6 Two separate circles, representing separate musical identities, but with emotional empathy

Reflecting

This technique is well documented in Bruscia's 64 techniques and he defines it as 'Matching the moods, attitudes, or feelings exhibited by the client' (Bruscia 1987, p.540)

In reflecting, unlike mirroring, copying or matching, the therapist's music might be quite different from the client's as the purpose of this therapeutic technique is to understand and reflect back the client's mood at that moment, rather than be a more technical reflection of their music. However, there needs to be congruence in mood or emotional expression between the therapist's music and the client's music otherwise the method would cease to have any empathic effect.

Conceptually, we can see two separate identities of the participants in reflecting (client and therapist), in a relationship where they are separated musically, yet still congruent emotionally. Figure 4.6 illustrates the separation of the therapist and client circles.

CD23 demonstrates a client playing in a random, rather directionless rhythm on percussion instruments (drum and cymbal). Note that the therapist allows a short time to pass before beginning to reflect musically and empathically. This is an important part of the process:

Listen to the client's music before giving a response.

I frequently find myself reminding students in training and therapists under supervision that reflecting on your experience of the client's music is essential to be sensitive in response. There are sometimes patterns or characteristics that can help both in deciding the therapeutic method of response and the musical 'style'. The response the therapist gives in CD23 reflects the aimless and random style of the client's playing, using melody and harmony.

CD Example 23: Reflecting example 1 – therapist on piano, client on drums and cymbal

In the next example, the client presents a very different picture while playing the piano. Feelings of anger and frustration are present in the sharp, bunched chords the client is playing. There is an underlying sense of pulse, with accents and sudden changes in dynamics to reinforce the apparent irritation of the client. The therapist reflects these feelings with a melodic line on the xylophone.

CD Example 24: Reflecting example 2 – therapist on xylophone, client on piano

Two exercises are now presented on the CD, with the client playing piano in the first and temple blocks in the second. While these examples do not allow the reader to understand the actual emotional state or feelings exhibited by the client, they can be used by imagining what they could be, based on the music that is presented and trying to find a way to frame a response that is an empathic reflection of the music.

Exercise: Using CD25 and CD26, listen to each example for a few seconds, establishing in your mind the possible emotional state or mood of the music ('client'), and then allow your own emotional state to be affected by the music you are listening to. When you have become sensitive to the mood or emotion present in the music you are listening to, and your own emotional reaction to it, begin to play that emotional reaction on another instrument, reflecting the feelings that are present in the music, and present in yourself.

CD Example 25: Reflecting exercise 1 – client on piano

CD Example 26: Reflecting exercise 2 – client on temple blocks

4.4 Grounding, holding and containing

Grounding, holding and containing are all therapeutic methods that are extremely useful when applied with clients who have a very random or floating way of playing, and way of being. It is helpful where the client appears or sounds unconnected to their music, or the music lacks any stability, direction or intentionality. I have defined the process of grounding as:

> *Grounding: Creating a stable, containing music that can act as an 'anchor' to the client's music.*

Examples of specific musical techniques that can be used in grounding include:

- strong octaves or fifths in the bass of the piano;
- steady pulsed beats on a bass drum;
- strong chords of a stable tonal nature using typically dominant and tonic chords;
- a simple ostinato.

Rhythmic grounding

Rhythmic grounding is a very useful way of providing a foundation to something the client is doing. Bruscia defines it as 'Keeping a basic beat or providing a rhythmic foundation for the client's own improvising' (Bruscia 1987).

Fig 4.7: Rhythmic grounding – client and therapist on bongos and bass drum

An important aspect of rhythmic grounding is that it is not necessary to impose a meter on the client's rhythmic musical production. In fact, it can be quite constraining and directive to take the client's musical production and establish a specific meter such as 4/4 or 3/4 for what they are doing. Music can be pulsed but meterless, and quite often becomes more dynamic by the variable use of accentuation within a stable pulse. Another important aspect is to intervene with a stable and secure melodic or rhythmic pattern, quite often limiting your playing where a client's playing is rather full and complex. The process of limiting in the therapist's music is to provide a stable and understandable ground, and avoid adding to the potentially chaotic complexity of the client's improvisation (Figure 4.7).

CD27 is an example of a client playing randomly on the xylophone, where the therapist then joins in on a drum and establishes a rhythmic ground to the client's music. You will hear the client begin to 'entrain' to the therapist's rhythmic ground and stabilize his or her own music accordingly.

CD Example 27: Example of rhythmic grounding – client on xylophone, therapist on a drum

---

Exercise: The next example on the CD (CD28) is a person playing a xylophone. Try to listen for any rhythmic patterns in the person's music, and then introduce a rhythmic ground. Remember, the faster or more complex the client's music, the more stable and limited must be the musical ground of the therapist. As this is an exercise requiring you to play with a CD example, potential for the person playing on the CD to 'adapt' to the therapist's grounding is clearly not expected. However it is a good exercise to practise finding ways of developing *matching* into *grounding.*

CD Example 28: Rhythmic grounding exercise client on xylophone

Tonal grounding

Tonal grounding is a process where one establishes a tonal bass which acts as a foundation or 'anchor' to the client's music if it is predominantly melodic or harmonic and is wandering around. I define this as:

> *Tonal grounding: Providing an octave, fifth or harmonic chord in the bass that is congruent with, and tonally grounding for, the client's music.*

Bruscia defines this as tonal centring – 'providing a tonal centre, scale, or harmonic ground' (Bruscia 1987, p.535).

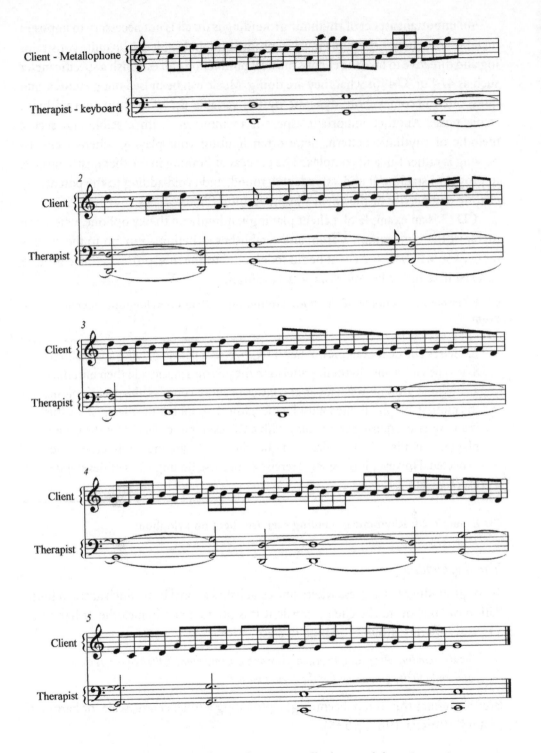

Figure 4.8: Example of tonal grounding – client on metallophone and therapist on piano

The musical example (Figure 4.8) illustrates this; a client plays a rather random, directionless melody on a metallophone which develops into repetitive patterns of falling thirds. The therapist intervenes with a tonal ground on the piano.

CD Example 29: Example of tonal grounding – client on glockenspiel, therapist on piano

---

Exercise: CD30 provides an exercise where a person plays music on a piano and as a duet partner you can work in the bass to provide some tonal centre for this. The technique involves analysing the type of music the person is playing and seeing if it falls within a key, or if a ground tone could be used as a tonal centre. For example, if the client is playing mainly the white notes of the piano, A minor, D minor and C major could be used as keys to provide a tonal centre. If the client is playing on the black notes, E flat minor and F sharp major can be used as the keys to provide the tonal centre (pentatonic).

CD Example 30: Tonal grounding – moving from diatonic to pentatonic

Harmonic grounding

Tonal grounding can be extended to *harmonic grounding*. This tends to involve either tonal harmonies (as in the two-chord improvisation) or pentatonic harmonies. As an extension to the use of fifths and octaves for tonal grounding, try using the CD30 exercise to engage with harmonic grounding.

Combined tonal and rhythmic grounding

Rhythmic grounding and *tonal grounding* can be combined to establish an even more secure musical foundation for a client. A good example of this would be to use a drone bass accompaniment figure to provide such a combined grounding foundation (Figure 4.9). The style could be given a 6/8 Celtic flavour by some suggestions from the therapist in the accompaniment, and then the harmonic ground can be enhanced with chordal structures (CD31).

CD 31 shows how the therapist maintains stability in the piano.

CD Example 31: Combined rhythmic and tonal grounding – client on piano, therapist also on piano

Holding and containing

Holding and containing are quite similar therapeutic methods. Basically, I employ holding as a therapeutic method and process where one provides a musical anchor to

Figure 4.9: Combined rhythmic and tonal grounding – client on piano and therapist on piano ground, even when there are mismatches in the harmony between the client's 'jumping around' melody and the drone ground

a client who is ungrounded in his or her playing and whose music is random and without direction. Consequently techniques such as tonal grounding/tonal centring are going to be helpful in order to provide that anchor. It works well to use simple harmonic accompaniments as a holding 'tool' where the use of sustained sounds without attempts at interactive or dynamic music making provides the containing frame. The therapist's music would typically be slow, sustained and very stable. However, at the same time it doesn't have to force a pulse or a meter on the client for it to be good enough music for holding. Therefore I define holding as:

> Holding: Providing a musical 'anchor' and container for the client's music making, using rhythmic or tonal grounding techniques.

Bruscia offers a different definition of holding, one that is more expanded to include the wider concept of the 'musical background', and also includes the concept that the technique contains the feelings of the client: 'as the client improvises, providing a musical background that resonates the client's feelings while containing them' (Bruscia 1987, p.536)

Containing implies a different process where the client's music is quite chaotic and may also be quite loud. Therapeutically, the client needs to be allowed to be chaotic, noisy, exaggerated (a good example would be an out-of-control child having a 'musical/emotional' tantrum). The therapist provides a musical container for the client's music, playing strongly and confidently enough to be heard by the client. One musical idea that can work well in therapy is to play at opposite ends of the piano with strong, stable octaves (CD32). Many other types of music could act as a container for the client's music, but it needs to be structured music that provides a pattern.

CD Example 32: Containing: Chaotic music contained by the therapist – client on cymbals, drums and xylophone, therapist on piano

4.5 Dialoguing

Music is a marvellous medium for engaging in different types of conversation or dialogue between two or more people. It is even possible, of course, to have a dialogue with oneself musically! I have not found a definition for *Dialoguing* in its application in music therapy as either a musical technique or a therapeutic method, although there are terms that describe some of the processes involved in making or developing a dialogue. I define dialoguing in the following way:

> Dialoguing: A process where therapist and client/clients communicate through their musical play.

There are two main forms of dialogue, which I define as follows:

> *Turn-taking dialogues: Making music together where the therapist or client(s) in a variety of ways, musical or gestural, can cue each other to take turns. This 'turn-taking' style of dialogue requires one or other to pause in their playing and give space to each other.*

> *Continuous 'free-floating' dialogues: Making music in a continuous musical dialoguic exchange – a free-floating dialogue. Here participants (therapist(s) and client(s)) play more or less continuously and simultaneously. In their playing musical ideas and dynamics are heard and responded to, but without pause in the musical process.*

To liken a dialogue to a conversation is probably the nearest and most understandable way of describing this process. Consequently, one can imagine that just as in a conversation, there are a number of ways in which the dialogue can progress:

1.   Therapist and client(s) take turns to play, taking over immediately from each other.

2.   Therapist and client(s) take turns to play with pauses in between 'statements'.

3.   Therapist or client(s) interrupt each other.

4.   Therapist and client(s) 'play at the same time' (talk at the same time) as each other.

5.   Client(s) make(s) long statements; therapist gives 'grunt' or 'ah-ha' responses of very short phrases.

6.   The therapist's musical style in the dialogue is very empathic (similar) to the style of the client(s) (or vice versa).

7.   The therapist's playing in the dialogue is very oppositional/confrontational to the client(s) (or vice versa).

Ways to promote dialogue

Musical dialogues don't necessarily occur automatically or naturally in improvisational music making. In fact, some clients find it extremely difficult to engage in dialogues, either because they can't follow or respond to normal turn-taking exchanges (typical in autistic clients), or because they talk so much that they don't stop for long enough to listen to what somebody else has got to say (this can be typical in clients with Asperger's syndrome).

Before explaining more specific techniques for promoting dialogue, there are two clearly defined therapeutic techniques proposed by Bruscia that can be utilized:

Interjecting – waiting for a space in the client's music and filling in the gap.

Making spaces – leaving spaces within one's own improvising for the client to interject his/her own materials (Bruscia 1987, p.535).

Using these two methods naturally leads one into dialoguing and initiates the 'conversation' or 'argument' style of improvisational music making, where the playing together becomes directly communicative. Many clients may not understand or pick up the signals that help nurture dialoguing, and this can be helped through modelling. Modelling is a method that can be applied to many of the previously described musical and therapeutic techniques, and many of those yet to be discussed. Bruscia's definition of modelling is:

Modelling – presenting or demonstrating something for the client to imitate (1987, p.535).

This provides us with a quite specific (and clearly directive) method which is most useful where that type of direction is needed. I would like to suggest an extended and broader definition here in order to explain that something more than purely imitating occurs:

Modelling: Playing and demonstrating something in a way that encourages the client to imitate, match or extend some musical ideas.

In the music making that goes on in music therapy there are subtle or obvious ways of promoting the initiation, development and progression of a dialogue. These involve either musical cues or gestural cues.

Musical cues

- Harmonic cues: indicating that you are coming to the end of some musical 'statement' by playing either a perfect or plagal cadence (or even an interrupted cadence). The harmonic modulation in a musical statement can also sound like a question.

- Rhythmic cues: playing a rhythmic pattern that closes, following which it is obvious that there is a space or playing a rhythmic pattern that is symmetrical and therefore gives a clear indication of closure (also allowing space for a client to play next).

- Melodic cues: playing in ascending phrase, a phrase that indicates the end of a pattern, etc.

- Dynamic and timbre cues: there are many types of dynamic cues that could indicate a space for developing a dialogue. Accents help to establish a punctuation point; making a crescendo on a phrase to a climax indicates a point of stopping; making an accelerando to a point of stopping also indicates a pause which allows a space for somebody to say something; staccato playing following some legato playing may also indicate something coming to a conclusion.

Gestural cues

Given that musical cues can be rather subtle and are not necessarily attended to, especially by clients who enjoy making a lot of noise and playing continuously, it may be necessary to model the dialogue idea through giving a gesture. The idea is to indicate a space where you would like the client to start playing (or continue playing) on their own in order to develop the dialogue. Therefore you can introduce some of the following ideas:

- Show you have stopped playing in some way, by taking your hands from the instrument or 'freezing' at the instrument so that you are not moving at all and looking as if you are waiting for the client to stop before you can play again (very effective with children when they catch on to the idea as it gives them a strong sense of being 'in control'!)

- Turn to look at the client and take your hands off the instrument.

- Use eye referencing to indicate that you are going to play and then eye reference the instrument to encourage the client to play.

- Point and indicate whose turn it is to play.

- Use physical prompts, either to encourage somebody to start playing, or to encourage them to stop playing:

  Starting to play:

  - nudging behind the elbow;
  - supporting under the elbow;
  - supporting under the wrist;
  - taking a hand and helping a client to play.

  (This is a graduated list of responses from a very gentle prompt to a hand-over-hand modelling.)

Figure 4.10: Example of Dialoguing – client on xylophone, therapist on congas

Stopping playing:

- putting the hand out in a stop position;
- reaching over and almost touching the hand of the client;
- reaching over and holding the beater or instrument that the client is using to play for a short time;
- reaching over and stopping the client playing physically by holding their hand; taking an instrument away while you interject a short phrase and then handing the instrument back.

(This is a graduated list ranging from gestural cues to physical direction.)

Figure 4.10 illustrates an emerging dialogue beginning with a client playing on a xylophone, without pulse, and shows how the therapist gently interjects, makes spaces for the client, then uses rhythmic patterns to develop the dialogue.

CD Example 33: Dialoguing 1– client on metallophone, therapist on xylophone

The techniques described above range from subtly to strongly directive. Direction in some form is sometimes necessary in order to build up, through modelling, the process of musical dialoguing or turn-taking. I am often asked how one can develop communicative musical dialogue with clients who have perseverative and repetitive playing, who seem to be unable or unwilling to leave any space in their musical production to allow a dialogue to develop. The ideas described above are typical in the techniques I have found helpful to model, initiate and develop dialogue. However, one also needs to take into consideration the instrument chosen and the physical playing style. Clients who play repetitive pulses on drums may do so because the motor movement (also described as sensory motoric playing) is what they are interested in doing, and there is little or no musical or communicative intentionality. All the above techniques may prove futile in the face of such playing, and changing instruments may be the best way to break down obsessive patterns of playing and introduce dialogue.

Phrasing, interrupting, pausing and talking at the same time

Having begun to develop dialogue, the patterns that emerge can sound more and more like a conversation when attention is paid to phrasing, interrupting, pausing and talking at the same time. Phrase lengths vary – especially where one person is doing most of the talking, and the other is merely acknowledging or confirming with an 'uh-huh' response. So, in musical dialogue, these patterns of conversation can increasingly represent the prosody and phrasing of speech, with accents, inflec-

Figure 4.11: Example of conversational dialogue using variable phrasing, continued on next page

Figure 4.11: Example of conversational dialogue using variable phrasing, continued

tion, interruptions and sometimes even talking at the same time. In the process of dialoguing – whether through a rhythmic or a melodic exchange – the potentials of varied phrasing will add significantly to the communicative character of the dialogue.

Figure 4.11 illustrates this, and CD Example 34 shows how all the dynamic aspects of interpersonal communication can be present in a musical dialogue. Given that music therapy is a medium through which 'communication' takes place through musical exchange, dialoguing is a very important and valuable technique to support and engage a client.

In the real world, communication and dialogue between people can frequently turn into a heated debate, perhaps even an argument. Polite turn-taking gives way to interrupting, increasing accents, 'rude' sounds, shouting, losing tempers – everything a good healthy argument should have! CD34 illustrates the musical dynamic of dialogue that becomes an argument, and as music therapy allows people to say something in music (in an argument) that would be unacceptable in words, this is a valuable tool in therapy work to draw out emotional attitude and affect.

CD Example 34: Dialoguing 2: Conversations and arguments! Therapist on xylophone, client on African split drum and djembe

Continuous 'free floating' dialogues

When working with clients who play quite continuously, repetitively, perhaps even obsessively, and have difficulty in stopping to listen, the therapist's option is to try to promote or engage with the second type of dialogue method described above – the continuous 'free-floating' dialogue. Here, the therapist can listen to and echo musical ideas, themes, motifs and dynamic patterns of the client, attempting to build up a dialogue of musical ideas within an ongoing improvisation.

It cannot be compared with a conventional conversation, where turn-taking is a typical element. In the free-floating dialogue, the musical genre of opera is represented, where two (or more) people can be simultaneously contributing to an exchange, sometimes singing about two different things at the same time, yet with a necessary musical connection through melody or harmony. It happens frequently in improvisations, and this kind of instantaneous reciprocity and shared understanding builds up between client(s) and therapist, and acts as a framework for communicative experiences. The subtlety of this type of interaction is such that it is not always possible to be aware of how it is happening while it is going on, and only with later audio or video analysis can one recognize the presence of a subtle and developing dialogue. CD35 gives an example of just such a dialogue, where the therapist uses the xylophone to match, and then dialogues with a client's continuous playing on a drum.

CD Example 35: Dialoguing 3: continuous 'free-floating' dialogue – therapist on piano, client on xylophone

4.6 Accompanying

Accompanying is one of the most useful and important of the supportive techniques in improvisational music therapy. I often recommend its use when one has established a framework for clients to use or where a client is particularly autonomous and wants to take a soloist's role in the music making.

I define the therapeutic method of accompanying as:

> *Accompanying: Providing a rhythmic, harmonic or melodic accompaniment to the client's music that lies dynamically underneath the client's music, giving them a role as a soloist (Wigram 2000b).*

Accompanying is a frequently used method for joining in with a client's music where the message one is giving is of support and empathy. The definition refers specifically to the idea that the music lies 'dynamically underneath', and this typifies the quality of 'accompanying' and gives it strength as a supportive music. If the client plays *f* then the accompaniment is going to be *mf*. If the client plays above middle C in the tonal range, the accompaniment can be placed lower, although it is possible to work with a bass lead and an accompaniment in the higher register.

Accompaniment style music, certainly on the piano, needs to have certain characteristics:

- to be simple and repetitious;
- to be a short rhythmic or harmonic sequence that is sustained;
- to continue in a stable way despite some changes in the client's music;
- to be sensitive to pauses or small developments in the client's music.

Typically, accompaniments can be (either tonal or atonal) um-cha-cha (3/4 waltz) style or um-cha-um-cha (2/4 and 4/4 common time) style. Figure 4.12 gives us an example of this type of accompaniment, in both a tonal and an atonal frame.

However, there are also some important other types of accompaniment. The 2-chord improvisation that was exemplified in Chapter 3 is a good sequence to use for an accompanying style, as is the Spanish 2–8-chord sequences that will be explained in Chapter 6 under frameworking techniques.

Figure 4.12: Example of 3/4 and 4/4 accompaniment style using tonal and atonal frame, continued on next page

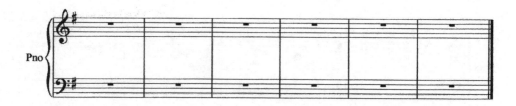

Figure 4.12: Example of 3/4 and 4/4 accompaniment style using tonal and atonal frame,
    continued

CD36 gives an illustration of a client starting to play randomly on a xylophone and glockenspiel while the therapist introduces an accompaniment style using (at first) two chords to support it, then developing some accompaniment effects.

CD Example 36: Accompanying – client on xylophone and glockenspiel, therapist on piano

Most of these accompaniment methods can be equally effective on guitar or other harmonic instruments (harmonica, accordion, autoharp, organ, synthesizer). Purely rhythmic accompaniments can also be generated, and are especially effective in providing a supportive frame. The most important characteristic of this therapeutic method to remember is your supportive role, allowing the client to take the lead, playing more softly, with stability and repetitious motifs of figures, and perhaps with a thinner, sparser texture.

Exercises: Try making different types of accompaniments to the following styles of playing using the examples on the CD with which to work:

CD Example 37: Accompaniment exercise 1 – a wandering treble melody by a client on a piano where they play first of all only on the white keys and secondly only on the black keys

CD Example 38: Accompaniment exercise 2 – a client playing an accented, rhythmic and pulsed melody on xylophone and metallophone, that breaks out of meter halfway through

CD Example 39: Accompaniment exercise 3 – a client playing some rhythmic patterns on a drum

---

In all three exercises try formulating accompaniments using different instruments such as piano, guitar or drums/percussion.

4.7 Summary and integration

These are some basic therapeutic methods that need to be practised in order to acquire both the technical and therapeutic skills to use them. As can be seen, they start to incorporate the musical techniques that are adapted to fit the intention of the method. The exercises suggested in Chapters 3 and 4 are designed to allow the reader a chance to practise these methods using either piano or other instruments. Many of these musical techniques and therapeutic methods will be revisited in later chapters because improvisation is not undertaken with clients through isolated methods, but through a sequence (sometimes fast-moving) of different methods and musical techniques.

The last part of this chapter is therefore concerned with the integration and sequential process of linking together these methods to illustrate how one can move through a therapeutic sequence of events with a client. As has been stated earlier, *matching* is a logical and empathic place to start with a client. However, in therapy we don't approach our clients with some predetermined plan of intervention, at least not in improvisational music therapy. The spontaneous experience, adapting and responding on a moment-by-moment basis to the interactive process, requires us to maintain a free-flowing flexibility in the application of therapeutic method.

The last example, illustrated only as audio example CD40, shows how one might move through three or more methods in an improvisational interaction with a client.

Matching $\longrightarrow$ Accompanying $\longrightarrow$ Dialoguing $\longrightarrow$ Containing $\longrightarrow$ Matching

The client is playing a xylophone, and begins with rhythmic, melodic fragments. The therapist matches, and the engagement begins. As the client grows more confident, the therapist takes the role of accompanist. A little further on, the therapist takes an initiative by making spaces and interjecting, and introduces the idea of dialoguing. The client works with this, but as the dialogue builds up dynamically to an argument, the therapist adapts to a containing approach. As the client's music loses some of its intensity and energy, the therapist follows and returns to a final empathic section of matching.

CD Example 40: Example of integrating therapeutic method and musical technique

So far, the techniques and methods recommended for both practising and developing within an improvisational model for use in clinical work have concentrated on identifying specific techniques using musical parameters and therapeutic method. Most of the examples and the exercises recommended have involved a form of improvisation where the music is spontaneously created, using some simple play rules.

Frequently, when working with musical material, one wants to develop a style of improvisation that fits something that the client may be doing or to create a particular type of musical frame for some specific purpose. I call this method of work 'frameworking'. In addition, we are constantly faced with the need to find ways of making changes in the music, making a transition from playing in one way to playing in another way. The development of these transitions is a critical part of music therapy skills (and in fact is used very widely by musicians, composers and others to connect together different types of music).

In order to move to the next stage of the process of developing improvisation skills, I will describe and give examples of both frameworking and transitions and then explain a number of exercises that can be used to develop these methods.

CHAPTER 5

Advanced Therapeutic Methods: Extemporizing and Frameworking

Introduction

The methods described in this chapter are applied in therapy work for more specific purposes, and have therapeutic implications regarding their use. Consequently, it is important to relate them to the therapeutic direction within a particular intervention with either a client or a group of clients. I will describe and then give examples of them, as well as exercises by which the underlying technique can be practised. The methods can be applied in various models of music therapy, ranging from client-centred music therapy to analytical approaches.

5.1 Extemporizing

Whereas improvising can be described as the process by which one spontaneously creates 'new' music, and the musical material does not rely on a pre-defined set of criteria or structures from music that is already composed, published or recorded, extemporizing employs quite a different model.

In *Collins English Dictionary* (1993), to extemporize is defined as '…to perform, speak or compose (an act, speech, piece of music, etc.) without planning or preparation'. I would extend this concept in terms of music and music therapy to the ability to improvise on some existing composed musical material, or in a known style.

In the entrance test for Aalborg University's music therapy programme, students are given a short 2–4-bar melody fragment in a specific style and are asked to 'continue to make up (improvise) a melody in the same style as the fragment'. This is very much what extemporizing is about and why it is such a useful technique, both as a musical exercise and skill, and also as a method in music therapy.

There are situations and clients with whom one works where the use of free or atonal improvisation might be considered inappropriate (perhaps even contraindicated), and the clients find it difficult to deal with freely developed and spontaneously created sounds for various different reasons. For example, it has often been said that elderly clients with senile dementia or Alzheimer's disease find atonal or free improvisation a difficult medium in music therapy and are much more attracted to working with structure and with songs that they know. Consequently, the ability to extemporize in a certain style, giving a starting point, is a very useful skill and technique for music therapists because it also offers the possibility to develop or make a transition from a known song or a piece of music into something more improvised and perhaps more personally expressive. At the same time, when one develops the extemporization, because it involves working within a style of a piece of music, it enables one to return to the original composition or song at moments when the client demonstrates any insecurity, confusion or resistance.

I would like to give a clear definition of what I mean by extemporization:

Extemporization: Improvising on some given musical material, or as a pastiche of a style of composition, maintaining the musical and dynamic characteristics of the style.

This requires an ability to develop a musical structure that is related to, and congruent with, an existing musical style given in a song, piece or musical example. The extemporized music is an extension of music where one is improvising 'in the style of' that music, using the same musical elements and staying close to the original material.

Techniques to develop this process and guidelines for the creation of an extemporization include:

- Notice carefully the harmonic and rhythmic structure of the music, and use them in the extended material.

- Choose the moment in the music where the extemporization can begin, for example, avoiding a perfect or a plagal cadence at the end of a 'verse' or 'section', interrupting the cadence and starting the extemporization.

- If the music is centred around the tonic, dominant and sub-dominant and mediant (minor) types of harmonies, use these structures in the extemporization while varying the melodic style.

- Incorporate slowing down, speeding up, getting softer and louder into the extemporization, as well as some pauses in the music.

- Use some of the principles of thematic improvisation to pick out parts of the musical material in the original music and make some specific developments, e.g. melodic phrases or rhythmic patterns.

- Practise moving back into the original music, for example going back in at the chorus section of a song, or halfway through a verse.

There are three examples on the CD that exemplify this process of extemporizing. First, I use the well-known sixteenth-century English song 'Greensleeves'. This song is in 6/8, in a minor key, and with a clear straightforward harmonic structure. (Extemporization is naturally easier when the harmonic structure is less complex.)

Figure 5.1 illustrates a melodic extemporization on the theme of Greensleeves, using the style and contour of the melody, while introducing some variations that allows one to incorporate improvisational technique, but within a safe structure. This can also be developed through singing.

In the first CD example (CD41), Greensleeves is played from the beginning, to establish the style and then, as the song comes to a conclusion, rather than finish on a perfect cadence, the cadence is interrupted to continue with an extemporization. Following that, small variations in the style of the music are made, varying texture, intensity and phrase lengths, while sustaining the type of harmony, characteristic melodic contour, tempo and general dynamics that were present in the original. At a certain point, I gently return to the original piece to bring the extemporization to a close. As can be noticed in this example, more space appears in the music, there are pauses and the music takes on a more reflective, wandering quality halfway through.

CD Example 41: Extemporization 1: 'Greensleeves'

For the second example, I have chosen a Danish folk tune/hymn to illustrate how to build an extemporization on the type of song that might be chosen by an elderly person. Here, the whole verse is played first, following which the extemporization develops using the style of the melodic phrases, but then transforms it into a more dynamic frame, adding some accents and excitement to the music, after which I close again by returning to the original style.

CD Example 42: Extemporization 2: Danish folk song – 'Nu titte til hinanden'

Example three uses some more rhythmic music, in this case the song 'Streets of London' which has been very well known. This song uses the cycle of 5ths in its harmonic structure, and at first I sustain this harmonic frame, while the extemporization occurs in the melody and rhythm. Then some developments occur in the harmonic direction, modulating, but finally returning back to the original harmonic frame of the song.

Figure 5.1: Melodic extemporization using 'Greensleeves'

CD Example 43: Extemporization 3: 'Streets of London'

A final, perhaps slightly amusing way to develop extemporizing was mentioned earlier, the use of 'pastiche' or playing in the style of a composer. There is no easy way to describe the musical techniques to be able to do this spontaneously. In fact, everyone develops favourite styles of playing on the instruments on which they feel most confident, and the elements of a particular style have to be expanded into improvisation and extemporization. I have chosen three favourite styles of my own to illustrate this technique, and have used tunes that are international and recognizable for CD examples 44, 45 and 46.

CD Example 44: 'Twinkle, Twinkle, Little Star' in a baroque style (and in the minor!)

CD Example 45: 'God Save the Queen'/'My Country 'tis of Thee' in a classical style (and in common instead of triple time!)

CD Example 46: 'Auld Lang Syne' in the ragtime style of Scott Joplin

Extemporizing, as a method, tends to be complex and demanding. Certainly, when using more tonal music, the practitioner needs to have a good understanding of and facility with using modulation and transposition and an understanding of chordal structure and tonal sequences. The cycle of 5ths is commonly used in many compositions, and can be employed in extemporization as well. It is equally important to remember that the skill of extemporizing is to use the existing material, stay true to the existing musical ideas and components but develop the creative 'improvising' process in the music. Therefore, many musicians and practitioners may find extemporizing a greater challenge to their musical (and therapeutic) skills than improvising, where one retains the freedom to invent and create music. However, the objective (and value), clinically, is to stay close to the material the client feels most comfortable with, while introducing the potential for the music to become more individually expressive and representational of the client's own feelings and ideas. Simply playing a song or piece that clients request from beginning to end, perhaps with the client playing along, does not allow them to represent their own feelings to as great a degree as they may need to in the music as they are confined by the performance, style and length of the song/piece. Extemporization is a very good alternative to using an existing piece of music or freely improvising.

5.2 Frameworking

The creation of some appropriate musical structure to enable a client to engage, or in response to a client's music, is a process I have found natural and helpful during improvising (intentionally or unintentionally), and is very relevant in music therapy practice where clients need, for one reason or another, a clear musical frame. I describe this method as *frameworking*, and will refer to it as a specific tool in music therapy practice that can be used quite precisely in treatment. A framework might have the function of inspiring and encouraging, or it might equally have the function of stabilizing and containing. The process by which one can develop abilities to use frameworking is explained in this section, and examples given. However, the therapeutic application of such methods is individual and idiosyncratic depending on the needs of the clients and the approach in therapy. As is the case so often with music therapy method and technique, a way of intervening – such as frameworking – can be described, but its application is down to client need and therapeutic judgment. The potential accurately to describe and prescribe procedural interventions in music therapy is limited – especially in improvisational music therapy.

My definition for this method is:

'Frameworking: Providing a clear musical framework for the improvised material of a client, or group of clients, in order to create or develop a specific type of musical structure.'
(Wigram 2000b)

The process involves creating a musical structure that can allow (and inspire) the development of more expressive and creative playing by the client.

Among the 64 techniques described by Bruscia, he offers the term 'Experimenting', explaining that it involves ' …providing a structure or idea to guide the client's improvising, and having the client explore the possibilities therein'. This is a more general definition, not specifically confining the method to a musical framework. I want to identify the process of frameworking as a music therapy method, and exemplify it musically.

Frameworking can be a directive or structuring technique in music therapy. It is not primarily empathic in its purpose, although the frame provided can be empathic to the feelings and mood of the client. Music therapists and improvisers generally have styles of music in which they feel both comfortable and skilled and it is quite typical that people make musical frameworks to give to clients in their music making that draw on their own strengths musically.

Listening to many of the recordings and styles of the work of one of the very great pioneers of music therapy, Dr Paul Nordoff, one can hear how clearly his own musical style of composition and the genre in which he is creating music appears in the musical material which he is using with the clients. There are many great examples of Nordoff providing a musical framework for a client's music that is clearly designed to inspire and stimulate their response. Consequently, their response does become more excited, more engaged with the music of the therapist and quite often more complex.

I often reflect that we have been trained in improvising and music making, and many of the clients with whom we work have not. Consequently, if the musical engagement stays at a purely mirroring or matching level, the degree to which they can become more expressive in their music making, and perhaps externalize their feelings and emotions, may also be limited. I have found in clinical work that frameworking, provided that it doesn't become over-dominant, is a marvellous technique for encouraging and exploring the musical and communicative expressivity of the client. Frameworking is used for specific purposes with specific clients (as in the case of extemporization), and there are good examples where providing a musical framework can help clients 'move on' (change and develop), or develop their expressivity in the way they are able either to make music or join in.

The process and method of initiating a framework involves a number of important stages. This is not intended as a step-by-step procedure, but offers a rough guide for the stages through which frameworking can be introduced, developed and then transformed or merged (through a transition – see Chapter 6) into a new section of the improvisation.

- Listen carefully to the musical production of the client and consider what type of musical frame would support it, or whether the client is already demonstrating the elements of a frame in his or her music.

- Analyse the style of the client's music to take into consideration a potential framework of harmony, melody and rhythm.

- Initially establish *matching* with the client's music.

- From matching, begin to develop a musical framework that can be used.

- At this point, reflect on whether the client's playing and the framework you are creating are relatively congruent in order for the client to feel his or her music is a part of the frame.

- Reflect on the client's response to the musical frame as to whether it is positive, neutral or negative.

- Note any ways in which the client begins to use the musical frame (or elements of it).

- When the client uses the musical frame, ensure that you drop down into a more supportive role using either accompanying as a method, or perhaps grounding/holding.

Techniques and styles

The musical techniques described in Chapter 3, in particular chordal improvisation, melody dialogues, tonal and atonal structures, dissonance, and the ideas of 6ths 3rds, triads and inversions are all types of framework. A wide range of musical genres and styles can be adapted as musical frameworks, and it would extend the length of this chapter (and book) by hundreds of pages to try to document the musical elements that constitute musical style in all these genres. From the classical tradition, styles developed from early music, where organum (playing with octaves and fifths) typical in the tradition of religious music developed into the polyphonic and contrapuntal styles of the rococo and baroque eras. Music became more ornamented, with increasingly complex harmonies. Musical form developed from the simplicity of binary and ternary, to sonata form, rondo and theme and variations. Composers adopted distinctive styles and, as has been explained in the previous section on extemporization, characteristics of those styles can be incorporated into a framework to give an experience of playing in the style of Haydn, Sibelius, Debussy or Britten. In music therapy, adopting the concepts of free improvisation has meant that we have used the principles of twentieth-century music, containing dissonance, atonality, a frequent lack of traditional musical form and spontaneous creativity within a thematic frame.

Using styles and characteristic from popular or folk music may be altogether more manageable. For example, it is easy to become familiar with the style of Elton John, which is nevertheless unique in the use of certain characteristic features in the harmony (i.e. plagal cadences using many sub-dominant to tonic modulations), and in the vocal style. Developing skills at playing in the style of rock, heavy metal, boogie woogie, swing, blues, gospel, calypso or ragtime, many of which have ethnic characteristics, relies at first on establishing an appropriate rhythmic structure, with accents and syncopation typical for the individual style. Harmonic variability is not very complex, sometimes with a limited selection of only four to five chords. The style is often determined by how you play, rather than complexity in the harmonic or melodic material. In the same way that there are subtle differences in the use of orna-mentation and counterpoint in Bach and Scarlatti, there are equally important differ-ences between bossa nova and pasodoble, even though both lie within a Spanish genre.

Frameworking is a flexible model where the characteristics of any style can be deployed. As explained in the process above, the introduction of a framework may come from therapist or client, and when continued in rigid or perseverative style can overwhelm and block the potential musical (and therapeutic) process of the client.

While frameworks are very useful in therapy, they also need to be introduced and applied with caution.

The chapter continues with three examples of frameworking based on three quite different styles of music making with which I feel familiar, and through which I can see the potential for structure and flexibility in improvisations. These styles of frameworking are also illustrated as musical examples in the text prior to each CD excerpt. Given the nature of spontaneous improvisation, the examples in the text and on the CD are not exactly the same, but similar in style to demonstrate the method.

5.3 Jazz frameworks

The first example uses a jazz style as a frame for a client's music. The rationale behind this, at a therapeutic level, may be quite specific for individuals with different patho-logical or social problems. From my own clinical experiences with clients who have autism and autistic spectrum disorder, their primary need is for a stable structure with which they can feel secure, and within which they can demonstrate their potential communicativeness and creativity. Jazz frameworks can provide this, and at the same time allow creative improvisation within the structure. In the first example of frameworking, I have incorporated three or four different styles:

- walking bass (atonal);
- walking bass plus syncopated chord structure (atonal);
- walking bass plus chord structures plus jazz melody (atonal);
- walking bass plus chords (tonal);
- walking bass plus chords plus melody (tonal).

Figure 5.2 gives an example of an atonal walking bass, which is then joined by atonal chordal structures (using quite widely spaced, 'open' chords) and then inter-spersed with atonal melody. Walking basses tend to be step-wise, with occasional 'skips'. For practice purposes, it is also wise to make sure that the tempo (pace) of this walking bass is steady and stable, and not fast. The chords used are also widely spread, rather than clustered, and almost never 'on the beat or half-beat'. A golden rule in both tonal and atonal improvisation is to include repetition of ideas, sequences and phrases to ensure that there is some direction and familiarity in the musical material.

CD47 demonstrates the idea of providing a jazz frame, where the client begins, using cymbal and xylophone. While the client's music is simple, and without much direction, what can be heard is a sense of pulse, giving the therapist the potential to

Figure 5.2: Framework 1: Atonal walking bass, with chords and melody

employ the jazz frame. Note how the client begins to pick up the ideas provided in the frame, and when confidence and expressivity develops, the therapist reduces the strength of his or her input to a more supporting (accompanying) technique and method.

CD Example 47: Frameworking: Atonal jazz framework – client on xylophone and cymbal, therapist on piano

Tonal frames in jazz improvisation provide a more secure and predictable musical sequence. There are some logical harmonic modulations in the 16-bar chord sequences illustrated in Figures 5.3 and 5.4, where the key sequence passes through subdominant, sub-mediant and supertonic to the dominant at the end of bar 8, and then back to the tonic again by bar 16. 1st and 2nd inversions are achieved by ensuring the bass octave does not always resort to the tonic root. The frame can typically be used when a client is playing on drums or other percussion instruments, but can also be applied successfully if a client is playing diatonically on the piano, xylophone, marimba or metallophone, or singing. Tonal jazz frames are considerably more structuring, and the therapist needs to be prepared for a client's lack of fluency, sometimes working flexibly with pauses in the client's music. There is a significant skill in being able to be flexible with tempo and with meter as, when a client 'falls out' of the structure (missing a beat, or varying tempo), adaptability is essential.

Figure 5.5 illustrates the use of the walking bass within one of these tonal frames. The direction of the walking bass now has to follow a defined harmonic structure, and there are a few more jumps in the walking bass in order to stay within the harmony of the jazz frame.

Figure 5.3: Tonal jazz framework example 1 – using a 16-bar harmonic pattern

Figure 5.4: Tonal jazz framework example 2 – using a 16-bar harmonic pattern

If clients are playing percussion instruments and xylophones, it is quite possible to incorporate other aspects of improvising using methods described previously, such as melody dialogues or rhythmic thematic improvisation. CD48 illustrates the walking bass that begins as an atonal walking bass with atonal chords and melody and then becomes more tonal, with a clearer chord structure.

CD Example 48: Frameworking: Tonal jazz framework – client on glockenspiel and metallophone, therapist on piano

5.4 Spanish and Latin American frameworks

Another inspiring musical style, ideal for use in improvisation, is Latin American or Spanish style. In a similar way to jazz, this introduces very clear aspects of synco-

Figure 5.5: Tonal jazz framework example 3 – a 16-bar harmonic pattern with walking bass

pated rhythm but it also includes much greater degrees of flexibility and deviation in the underlying pulse, as one often finds in Spanish music with frequent use of rubato, hiatus and fermata.

To practise in a Spanish style, I recommend initially using the two-chord model. This is exemplified in Figure 5.6, where the recitative style of two-chord improvisation illustrates the potential for using many types of melodic figures typical in Spanish Latin music. Initially, one should try this on the piano using a recitative style of playing, placing the chord in the left hand and developing a right hand melody and then randomly changing the chord in the left hand *outside* any type of regular pulse. I suggest particularly the use of repeated notes, ornaments such as 'turns', mordents and appoggiaturas, as well as sequences and scale passages using the types of scales typical in the Spanish harmonic style (see Figures 5.7 and 5.8).

A xylophone or metallophone can be set up with a Spanish scale (i.e. Figure 5.7), but the fascinating complexity of the harmonies in Spanish music often relies on two different scales used at the same time, as illustrated in both Figure 5.8 and CD49, which demonstrates the two-chord style, using the chords and scales described in Figures 5.6, 5.7 and 5.8.

CD Example 49: Spanish improvisation – recitative, going to pulsed

From the simple beginning of using two chords (Figure 5.8), incorporating further elements, harmonic, rhythmic and melodic, develops and builds up the style. A pulse and meter can then be established, and the improvisation can develop to include further chords (Figure 5.9).

CD50 demonstrates how this can be developed using a variety of different Spanish accompaniment rhythmic figures (Figure 5.10).

In this genre it is important to note how slurring chords or melody over bar lines increases the sense of syncopation that is so typical in Spanish music. The power of melody comes very much into play in Spanish style with variability using ornamentation and embellishment. CD50 demonstrates Spanish-style melodic and rhythmic frame to the music of a person playing something relatively simple on a bongo drum.

CD Example 50: Spanish improvisation – with tempo and meter – client on bongos, therapist on piano

Figure 5.6: Two-chord Spanish improvisation – recitative style

Spanish scale

Figure 5.7: Spanish scale

Figure 5.8: Two Spanish scales used for the chords in Figure 5.6 and the CD50 example

5.5 Modal frameworks

The third style I have chosen to illustrate frameworking demonstrates the use of a modal type of frame where I have reduced the influence of rhythm. In the example (Figure 5.12) a client is playing rather randomly on the keys of a metallophone and the frame applied by the music therapist is intended to give a harmonic ground without imposing any form of rhythmic structure on it. The example employs three specific scales – the Dorian, Ionian (major) and the Aeolian (Figure 5.11), which provide a modal quality to the music. Pentatonic scales are also useful to create a modal quality in improvisation, and two pentatonic scales are also illustrated in Figure 5.11.

The CD example (CD51) begins without any clear structure. As the music develops and the modal frame provided by the therapist on the piano begins to incorporate the element of melodic phrasing in order to evoke more structure and expression in the music, the client engages with the ideas in the musical frame. Subsequently, the therapist begins to introduce accents and variability in volume in the music. This type of frame is intended to shape many aspects of the client's music. Rhythmical shaping, harmonic shaping and dynamic shaping could also be defined as methods by which one gives an expressive shape to material that a client is producing.

CD Example 51: Modal frameworking – Client on metallophone, therapist on piano

Figure 5.9: Spanish improvisation – with tempo and meter and additional chords

Figure 5.10 – Some Spanish rhythmic figures

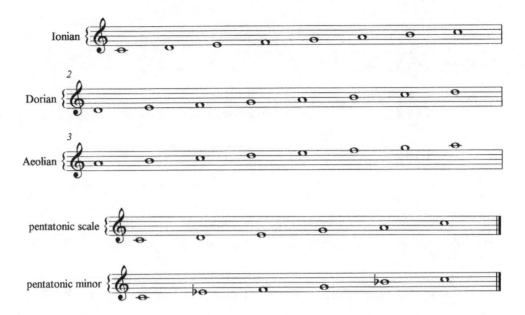

Figure 5.11: Ionian (major), Dorian and Aeolian scales and two pentatonic scales

5.6 Summary

I feel it's important enough to restate that while frameworking (and extemporizing) can be used as directive and structuring methods of music therapy, providing a strong lead to the clients (perhaps even suggesting to them they could play in a certain way) the most important aspect to remember is that the framework is given to the clients in order for them to be able to incorporate and develop their own music within it. For various reasons, one might experience resistance from the client to a frame and perhaps even an active rejection of the frame musically. Then the therapist should consider abandoning one frame in order to have some space before beginning to offer a new frame. It may also be that the client is unable to respond to, or understand the musical frame, or is overwhelmed by it.

Essentially, the frame is there to offer the client inspiration and creative ideas, and when they start to use those creative possibilities, the therapist must remember to drop down to a more supportive, accompanying role and be satisfied that by using frameworking as an intervention they have engaged some important potentials in the client.

Figure 5.12: Modal frameworking – client on metallophone, therapist on piano

Figure 5.12: Modal frameworking – client on metallophone, therapist on piano, continued

Figure 5.13 Tonal framework for 1-note improvisation (David Wigram), continued on next page

Figure 5.13 Tonal framework for 1-note improvisation (David Wigram), continued

Personally, I have found it a very useful method to use with clients where musical material can be rather limited and perhaps even repetitive and boring. People with severe learning disability, depression, or with very repetitive ways of playing can all be inspired and engaged by a musical frame that is more aesthetically satisfying. As a final example (Figure 5.13) a recent composition by the youngest member of my own family drew on an idea similar to that used by Chopin in the 'Raindrop' Prelude (Opus 28, No. 15), with a single repeated note. The composer here created a frame that placed the production of the 'client' (the repeated note) onto the off-beat, and then created a melodic and harmonic structure congruent with the repeated note. While the repeated note was not changed, the composition enfolded this tone into a structure and built a framework around it.

CHAPTER 6

Transitions:
In Improvisation and Therapy

Transitions and the use of transitional material in improvisational music making are probably the most useful and important methods I have developed in clinical work for the development of improvisation skills. Music rarely stays the same; it develops, changes and transforms. The period during which music changes, whether it lasts for two seconds or five minutes, I call a transition. The process of changing and developing musically with clients in a musical engagement is critical in the music therapy relationship, particularly in terms of what it represents. In this chapter, I define and exemplify different types of transition based on how they occur, and what elements they contain.

Bruscia describes making transitions as 'having the client find various ways within an improvisation to go from one quality or feeling to its opposite' (Bruscia 1987, p.536). In using and identifying transitions in music making and clinical improvisation, as well as in the therapeutic process, I have expanded this for more general and wider application. Transitions can be subtle or overt, long or short, progressive or regressive – in fact there are many aspects of transitions where musical and therapeutic process complement each other,

Of particular note both for musicians who improvise music and music therapists who use improvised music in clinical work with clients is that it is very easy for music to become stuck, blocked, repetitive and unchanging. The process of improvisation can result in client and/or therapist going round in 'musical circles'. This is particularly noticeable where the pathology of a client (such as depression, anxiety, autism) also results in unchanging patterns of behaviour. Transitions are the 'antidote' to a lack of movement and change, both in music making and in therapy work.

6.1 Definition of transitions

Transitions – The process by which the music of the therapist and the client(s) moves from one musical framework to a new musical framework (Wigram 2001).

Supplementary elements can be added to this definition:

An element/elements in the music is/are changed, either by client or therapist, to introduce a change in the musical dynamic in order to facilitate movement and change in the shared music making. This process can represent, or act as a catalyst for, change and movement in the personal life or therapeutic process of clients (Wigram 2001).

The term 'musical framework' has here a different meaning from that defined in 5.2 where I am talking about frameworking more in the context of how the therapist will introduce a specific style as a musical framework. Here, the creative music of a client (together with the therapist and/or other clients) includes a variety of different musical elements and structures, which can be referred to as the 'musical framework'. Any changes in those elements or musical structures will result in the creation of a new musical framework.

A transition can be a simple process of changing one small aspect of the musical material. (This will be referred to later where I describe a particular type of transition called a 'seductive transition'.) Listening to improvisations both when students learn improvising skills and when improvisation is used in clinical work, one can be aware and impressed by how little change there is in the music at a dynamic, rhythmic or tonal level. In fact, music can get into a rut, or a pattern that seems to be unchanging. Small changes I define as 'simple transitions' where the music simply moves by means of manipulating or changing one small aspect of the musical material, while all other aspects stay the same. A number of useful 'simple transitions' are illustrated in Table 6.1.

Table 6.1 Simple transitions

Musical dynamic

Non-accented	....	Accented
Staccato	....	Legato
Loud volume	....	Soft volume
Thick texture	....	Thin texture
High pitched	....	Low pitched
In phrases	....	Continuous

Rhythm and tempo

Slow	....	Fast
Non-pulsed	....	Pulsed
Common meter	....	Waltz
Rhythmically stable	....	Rhythmically chaotic

Tonality, melody and harmony

Step-wise melody	....	Melody with large jumps
Tonal	....	Dissonant
Tonal	....	Atonal
Atonal	....	Pentatonic
Major	....	Minor
Pentatonic	....	Chromatic

To develop skills in simple transitions isn't difficult, and it's quite fun.

Exercise: Choose a favourite piece of music, play it in the style in which it's supposed to be played and then, using the list in Table 6.1, introduce a dynamic, tempo or tonal change in the music that just involves using one of these elements.

Exercise: Improvise in a pentatonic style (using the black notes of the piano) in a 4/4 meter, placing an accent on the first of every four beats. Then reduce the accent to almost nothing until you have an accentless, meterless type of music and then reintroduce an accent on every third beat, re-establishing the meter as a waltz. Go backwards and forwards between a waltz (3/4) and a common meter (2/4 or 4/4) style of playing using the music you have created.

Exercise: Use some of the basic improvisation skills defined in Chapter 3. For example, begin a tonal melody dialogue on the white notes of the piano and start to explore small changes through simple transitions going from using tempo, rhythm, musical dynamic or tonality.

Exercise with a partner: Ask your partner to begin playing, following which you initiate matching with them. Then initiate a simple transition using one of the above processes (or others you may think of).

These are basic methods in developing simple transitions, involving a gradual change in the music from style A to style B. However there are more specific and applied types of transitional methods that I have found useful, and subsequently defined in my own clinical and research work. They are as follows:

- Seductive transitions;
- Limbo transitions;
- Overlap transitions.

These three methods are addressed in the next three sections and there will be exercises and CD examples to illustrate them.

6.2 Seductive transitions

This method follows on quite naturally from the idea of simple transitions because it involves a small change in the musical material, and therefore it is the most practical to learn. Seductive transitions (and the 'seduction' referred to can be manipulated either by the client or the therapist!) involve a quite gentle and subtle process of change. I have defined seductive transitions as:

> *Seductive transition: Moving from one style of playing to another in such a gradual and gentle way that neither client nor therapist can tell exactly how or when the style changed.*

It is like looking at a paint chart in a paint shop, where the colour grey goes very gradually from a deep, dark grey through all the different blues in the spectrum of that colour to the very lightest grey. Typically, the change is not sudden or dramatic.

Figure 6.1: Paint chart – dark to light

Therefore, going from slow to very slow, from soft to very soft, from unaccented to very slightly accented are good examples of seductive transitions. In particular, the change that occurs may only apply to one aspect of the musical material while the other elements may not change and remain constant. This is the most effective way of changing the music from one style to another in a subtle and careful way.

The application of these is particularly helpful for clients where there is a strong resistance to change (such as clients with autism or problems of neurotic anxiety) or for musicians where making sudden and dramatic changes in the music is destabilizing. As soon as the new style is established, it is important to establish a period of stabilization, even when the change has been relatively small or limited.

In its most effective form, a seductive transition is a process where one cannot be absolutely sure where the change occurred. Consequently, the introduction of any type of change in the music needs to be approached very gently and subtly, otherwise the message that comes across musically is much more obvious and perhaps even directive.

This is demonstrated on CD52 where an example of a gentle and subtle transition in the shared playing between a client and a therapist moves very gradually from mezzo-forte to mezzo piano, and subsequently from continuous to music with some spaces.

CD Example 52: Seductive transition – client on conga drums, therapist on Chinese temple blocks.

It is important not to provoke change that is either dramatic or too fast through this type of transition. In fact, when working with clients who are either very resistant or hyper-sensitive to change, I notice that I work through a sequence of seductive transitions, establishing and stabilizing a new style of playing, before moving into another gentle period of change. I am informed by Kate Hevner's Mood Wheel here (Hevner 1936), where moving from tragic to happy would be an incongruent and insensitive mood change. Instead, one has to work around the wheel, from tragic to melancholy, melancholy to sentimental, sentimental to lyrical, lyrical to whimsical, and finally from whimsical to happy. The seductive transition method can be used when it is necessary to be cautious and discreet in working towards therapeutic change.

Exercise: Begin a two-chord improvisation with a melody in the right hand and introduce very gradually a transition where the music moves from being pulsed to non-pulsed. This is actually one of the most difficult transitions to make as once a pulse has been established in music it's sometimes incredibly difficult to lose it. This is particularly so when you note that various aspects of a person's physical behaviour are associated with the pulse and, even when their body isn't moving to a pulse, they may still continue to experience a mental perception of it. However, try a gradual transition to disrupt and disturb the pulse in a subtle way, leading to a more non-pulsed style of playing.

These exercises work much better when tried out with a colleague in a duet experience, as it helps to reflect together on the effectiveness and subtlety of the transition that occurred and how both either cooperated in or resisted the process.

Exercise: Try using an improvisational technique that is easy and fluent for you and doesn't present any technical problems – such as playing a pentatonic improvisation on the black notes of the piano – and then introduce the following small changes:

- mezzo forte to piano;

- melodic to chordal;

- unphrased music to phrased music (with spaces in it).

6.3 Limbo transitions

The second type of transition I define is a limbo transition, because it involves going into a musical 'limbo' as part of the process of change. A limbo is defined in the dictionary as '…an unknown intermediate place or condition between two extremes: in limbo… ' (Collins English Dictionary 1993). There are other definitions, but it is this one that I am using in order to describe a 'limbo' transition.

The concept of limbo transition comes from the idea that within an improvisation (and within a therapy process) in order to explore the possibility of change, we may not know quite where to go or what to do, so we can drift into a 'limbo' state while trying to find out the new direction for a musical improvisation (or therapeutic direction).

Therefore, I have defined a limbo transition as:

Limbo transition: Moving from one style of playing to another through a musical 'limbo' where there is no definite musical direction, intention or purpose.

The experience of limbo is sustaining a moment or period of time of 'waiting', waiting to see what the client wants to do next musically, or waiting to see what the therapist could or should do next. It is a space, perhaps even a vacuum, from which anything could happen, or maybe nothing. There can be feelings of tension, of anticipation, expectation, confusion, of being lost, of a lack of pressure or demand, floating and perhaps even a sensation of not having to think or feel at all.

A musical 'limbo' is created by using transitional musical material that is repetitive and simple such as:

Figure 6.2: Repeated note limbo

Figure 6.3: Held chord and note limbo

- a repeated note;
- a repeated chord;
- a held note or chord (with a pause);
- a repeated melodic fragment;
- a rocking octave;
- a simple and rather circular sequence of notes.

Figures 6.2, 6.3 and 6.4 give musical examples of limbo material, where I have included a short section of 'before and after' music in order to provide the musical context in which the limbo transition occurs.

A musical and therapeutic limbo can be initiated and developed in various ways, and the following are some guidelines on how to go into them (and get out of them!).

- Going into the limbo can originate with either the therapist or the client.
- A limbo can last five seconds or five minutes.

Figure 6.4: Repeated melodic fragment limbo

Figure 6.5: Rocking octave limbo

- The single most important quality in a limbo is the feeling that the music has lost direction and isn't going anywhere.

- A limbo can also be accompanied avoiding obvious cues or non-verbal gestures that might give a message to a client that he or she should find a new direction.

- Limbo material can come out of the improvisational material.

- Limbo material can be unrelated to the improvisational material and just a musical device.

- There can be a gradual introduction of a new musical direction (signalled by a suggestion from either the client or therapist of a new musical idea).

- There can be a sudden introduction of completely new material as a result of being in an empty space.

- The client may choose to return to the style of playing he or she had just left.

- The improvisation may come to an end.

CD53 provides a demonstration of a limbo transition where the sense of losing direction is very clear in the material and is followed by the gradual introduction of a new musical direction. The music is pulsed and rhythmic at first, tonal and with a sense of meter. Then the two players move into a limbo that just uses and repeats one or two notes, loses a sense of pulse, and more space occurs in the music. The new musical direction begins to sound like an atonal dialogue, with random, atonal exchanges, no pulse or meter, and with staccato accented notes.

CD Example 53: Limbo transition – client on xylophone, therapist on piano

There are many occasions when going into a limbo in the musical improvisation does not necessarily result in either the client or therapist moving into 'new' music. It is often the case that clients choose to return to the style of music they have just left, preferring the security of a familiar way of playing and engaging to the unknown risks of some new material. In this case, a transition is entered, but a recapitulation occurs.

The improvisation could also have ended in the limbo material, as the process of going into a therapeutic limbo doesn't necessarily expect or demand that clients or therapist have to find a way out of it and go in a new direction. The improvisation might just 'fizzle out' … and this may be an important (pivotal) moment in the therapy.

There are many different ways in which you can practise limbo transitions. Again, the most valuable way is to ask somebody to play with you, draw them into a limbo and then practise finding a new direction. Many of the exercises in previous chapters can be used again, incorporating a limbo transition inside the experience.

Exercise: To practise the technique of using limbo transition, here is an exercise to employ some of the guidelines given above. It can be used as a model, with variation in style, limbo material, and new music. It is also good practice to enter the limbo *without* a pre-determined plan for the type and style of the 'new' music.

Step 1 – Decide on a style of playing that you want to use, such as atonal, pulsed with a melody in the right hand and chords in the left hand.

Step 2 – Decide on a new tone of music that is different from the first type of music, for example, legato, tonal, melody dialogue on the white notes only.

Step 3 – Decide on a type of limbo material from the list above that you could use.

Step 4 – Practise starting with the first music style, going into a limbo, and then initiating (suddenly or gradually) the second musical style.

Clinical application

Limbos are very useful in therapy work. They provide 'thinking time' that is necessary for reflecting on where therapist and client have been and need to go. Particularly when playing in pulses and with structured music (for example in frameworking), limbos can be very useful in allowing space to reflect on what is happening – to allow an 'external personal supervisor' to look down on the therapist's and client's engagement and therapeutic process, and say 'what's going on here?'. I find myself using this type of transition very frequently, even if the limbo lasts only 10 seconds. It can literally be 'marking time' (an old military expression meaning marching on the spot) musically and therapeutically.

Finally, its great value is that it is a place where one not only loses direction but perhaps also loses a sense of control. Of course, limbos can still be quite rhythmic (if a rhythmic pattern of notes is used and a pulse is sustained) but they can also be without pulse, with limited rhythm and very vague tonality and harmony. As such, they are very much an empty musical space acting as a transition and connection to a new musical space. It is worth realizing that classical composers were masters of the art of limbo transitions. Here are a few well-known examples:

1. Ludwig van Beethoven: Fifth Piano Concerto – second to third movement. Four bars before the end of the slow movement, a long note is held first in the bassoon, then in the horn, while the piano begins (two bars before the end) very slowly to introduce the theme of the last movement, subsequently played strongly.

2. Max Bruch: First Violin Concerto – first to second movement. Here the orchestra gradually come off the climax at the end of the first movement, getting slower and softer, until the strings just hold one note (B♭), leading us into the romantic and melodic second movement.

3. Edward Elgar: *Enigma Variations* – the connections between the eighth and ninth (Nimrod) variation. Again, as the eighth comes to a slow halt a note is held in the strings, for a marvellous inharmonic change from the tonic chord (G major) to the flattened mediant (E♭ major), introducing the new theme.

4. Franz Schubert: Unfinished (eighth) Symphony, first movement. Here, in bar 38, there is a clever little transition from the first theme to the second theme, with a note held through (again on the horns and bassoons), whereupon the clarinets and violas (bar 42) introduce a repetitive accompanying figure to provide both a transition and a frame for the new theme.

5. César Franck: Symphony in D, first movement. Franck uses a little limbo transition just before the end (bars 460–472) The music slows, loses direction, there are pauses, repeats of small parts of the main theme, and it slows to a complete halt (bar 472) Then the tempo (bar 473) rushes us towards the climax with a massive crescendo.

6. Hector Berlioz: *Symphonie Fantastique*, 'Dream of a Witches' Sabbath'. The transition between the opening Larghetto and the Allegro, where the time almost doubles (63–112), is managed by a repeated triplet C first in flutes and oboes, and then in the horns over 4 bars – creating much tension.

6.4 Overlap transitions

The third transitional method I have defined, and which has emerged from clinical experiences, is where one creates an overlap between one form of musical engagement and another. This is useful for both client and therapist because it is a clearer way of introducing a new type of musical idea while continuing with an existing way of playing. Therefore, overlap transitions are literally where musical material overlaps! I have defined them in the following way:

Table 6.2 Complex overlap transition – consecutive change in the individual musical elements			
Musical style A			Musical style B
Beginning	**1st stage of overlap**	**2nd stage**	**Final stage**
pentatonic	pentatonic	*atonal*	*atonal*
without pulse	without pulse	without pulse	*with pulse*

Overlap transition: Moving from one style of playing to another by introducing change in the elements of the music where a new element is introduced while the original style of the music is sustained. There is an overlapping of musical material.

Introducing a change to one element of the music enables one to go either forward or back, and the change can be initiated by either the therapist or the client. Subsequent changes in musical elements enable one to complete a process of change from one musical style to another.

An example of how an overlap transition works can be seen in Table 6.2. The above example shows how the material changes from music that is pentatonic, lacking in any pulse and smooth (legato) to music that is atonal, pulsed and staccato. Other elements of the music may also be changed but they are not specified. It is very clear from looking at the beginning and the final stage that there is a significant difference between these two styles of music. However, to make the jump directly from Music A (pentatonic, legato without pulse) to Music B (atonal, pulsed staccato) would be a very dramatic change. Attempting it one stage at a time allows either therapist or client to go *back one stage* if the element that has been introduced has been rejected by the client, or where the new style feels incongruent or innapropriate. For example, in the illustration above, if the introduction of staccato playing in the first stage achieved no response from the client and actually appeared to disturb him or her, one could easily withdraw it, reverting to the original type of music before introducing a new change. This idea of being able to go back to the original music is important in a number of situations:

- The client shows he or she is uncomfortable at the change.

- The client doesn't appear to register, hear or understand the change.

- The therapist feels the new idea is incongruent or inappropriate (a good idea that didn't work – otherwise known as a mistake!).

- The therapist can sense that the client isn't ready for that kind of change, and needs to explore another possibility.

The idea of overlapping is that a new element is introduced while the original material is sustained. A dramatic example could be playing legato, smooth chords in the lower part of the piano and introducing a staccato melody in the right hand while sustaining those chords in the left hand.

To put this method into practice, I would normally start by listening to the music the client is making, engage with them by matching or copying, and include all the stylistic elements of their music in my own – an empathic process. Then I have to decide what element I could influence to change first. This depends very much on knowing the client and the focus of therapy. With some clients, attempts to change fixed or rigid tempo is the last thing I might try, whereas with others, a change to the intensity of the music or its texture could also be a mistake. Some might argue that intervening in this way – introducing a change to the music as an overlap, is quite challenging and directive. As usual, the decision is a therapeutic judgment, but I have found that taking risks is part of therapy work, and the client(s) may well not understand how to change, or take the initiative to change. We are trying to promote, elicit and respond to music that represents an expression of personality, emotional expression and mood in the client.

It is equally clear from clinical experience that changes in musical elements and style, causing an overlap transition to occur, are initiated by clients, and need to be noticed and responded to by the therapist. Sometimes it is not always clear what clients are intending, or whether the change they have initiated is even consciously intentional. Beside supporting the change they have introduced, I will sustain the foundation we have built, until the new idea begins to develop.

Overlap transitions are the most explicit, and perhaps directive, of the transitional methods I have described – they make it fairly obvious that either you, or the client, want a change. CD54 gives an example of an overlap transition and shows the way in which the music is transformed from music A to music B. The music begins with an atonal harmony, accents, and with big jumps in the music. The range

Table 6.3 Complex overlap transition – exercise 1

Pentatonic	}		{	No pulse
Fast	}	going to	{	Melody in the right hand
Staccato	}		{	Slow

Table 6.4 Complex overlap transition – exercise 2

Tonal	}		{	Staccato
Waltz	}	going to	{	With pause
Slow	}		{	Atonal
Tune in right hand – then change	}		{	Chords

Table 6.5 Complex overlap transition – exercise 3

Fast	}		{	Waltz style
Melody in both hands	}	going to	{	Chords
No Pulse	}		{	Pulse
Dissonant	}		{	Pentatonic

Table 6.6 Complex overlap transition – exercise 4

Slow	}		{	Pentatonic
Tonal	}	going to	{	Waltz/dance
Short melodies/themes	}		{	Pauses

Table 6.7 Complex overlap transition – exercise 5

Tonal/melodic	}		{	Accented
Non-pulsed	}	going to	{	Pulsed
Unaccented	}		{	Dissonant

becomes more limited (change 1), the music becomes tonal and diatonic (change 2), the music stabilizes on a pulse, incorporating a waltz meter (change 3).

CD54: Overlap transition – client on glockenspiel, therapist on piano

---

Exercises: The following transitions in purely musical material can be practised using the overlap transition method.

6.5 Alternative frameworks for transition techniques

The methods described above give primarily musical frames with musical techniques for developing skills in making transitions using these three defined methods. There is also an interesting way of using other thematic material such as emotions, stories, pictures or themes for exploring transitions.

Transitions using emotions, feelings or moods

Previously, I have discussed the possibility of making thematic improvisation based on emotions or feelings and have given the example of going from one feeling, mood or emotion to another. This is a good exercise in which to include and develop the process of using transitions. The examples offered in Table 6.8 can be used as exercises in making transitions. Again, it would be sensible to pick emotions that aren't too widely differentiated for practice purposes.

Table 6.8 Exercise for making a transition from one emotion, mood or way of being to another

Emotional mood	Transitional method	New emotional mood
Insecurity	Limbo	Stability
Melancholy/sad	Seduction	Determination
Frustration	Overlap	Anger
Anxiety	?	Peace

I have found that in clinical work, and in teaching, when working with either emotional themes or pictures, therapist and client, or teacher and student, can approach the experience in two ways:

- Objective Emotional Representation (OER): Using programme music making to create music that you imagine best represents the emotion, feeling or image.

- Subjective Emotional Representation (SER): Experiential music making that involves preparing yourself/reminding yourself/placing yourself into the feeling or image either by recalling a recent event that rekindles the emotion of the experience, or actually experiencing the emotion in the here-and-now, and then playing what you are experiencing.

Table 6.9 Stories with transitions: 3 examples

	Story section 1	Story section 2	Story section 3
Example 1	You are floating on a calm lake. It is a hot, sunny day. Nobody is there.	The weather gets bad – there is suddenly a big storm.	You dive to the bottom of the lake – it is dark and blue, and cold. You find a cave, and go to sleep there.
Example 2	You are in a dark room. There are some dangerous animals in the room.	A white, friendly figure comes and takes you outside. The figure wants to dance with you.	A demon comes and carries you off. The white friendly figure rescues you.
Example 3	You are climbing up a high mountain, all the way to the top.	At the top you look at the panorama, then jump off and fly around.	You land in a fairground, and there are lots of people shouting and laughing.

These two 'ways in' are important to try, and either can be used dependent on the therapeutic situation. For example, I have tried using SER in my assessment work with children and adolescents with autistic spectrum disorder (ASD). I try to get them to remember a situation or recent occurrence when they experienced a particular mood or emotion. Once they have recalled something, or tell me that they are starting to feel in a certain way, I encourage them to play that feeling – in the here-and-now. This is difficult for people with ASD, who have poor imaginative play and impairments in their ability to represent symbolically.

We can create music in a more objective way to symbolize a feeling or promote a specific mood (OER). This can emerge as a rather technical exercise, sometimes employing musical stereotypes, such as loud crashing chords for 'anger' or soft wandering melodies with falling phrases to suggest loneliness or sadness. But one thing worth remembering is that if you ask five people each to play the feeling 'anger' you will certainly get different musical forms of 'anger'. People are different, their emotions are different, and the way they express those emotions also differs. Therefore, the second method of asking someone to engage with the feeling, and then (without thinking too much about how they are playing) to *play* the feeling they are in contact with, will probably result in a more genuine and authentic musical externalization of that feeling.

Transitions using stories and fantasies

A second framework is to construct a story or a fantasy journey through which one can travel musically, or a picture from which themes and concepts can be selected, and connect the ideas with transitions. This can be used as a teaching tool because it gives a more concrete representation to the musical material and allows the transitions to have a specific place in between sections. The story needs to be in two or three stages or steps, and transitions occur between them.

Exercise:

- Select a picture you like, and that has some interesting and different aspects to it.

- Look carefully at it and pick out three elements from the picture that have meaning for you. Those three ideas can be quite concrete; for example, the elements in the picture might include figures, landscape, buildings, action of some sort, or the picture could be quite abstract in terms of the impression that it is giving, such as a feeling of fear, a new direction or satisfaction.

- Place those elements in a specific order (perhaps a logical order or an order that might make a symbolic or metaphoric representation of the meaning of the picture).

- Think a little bit about the type of musical material you might use to represent these three issues in the picture.

- Begin the improvisation and use one of the three types of defined transitions (seduction, limbo, overlap) to go through the two transitions that will occur between these three elements of the picture.

Pictures also form effective media for both transitions and themes for improvisations, and I have often used them in teaching, as well as using images in therapy work.

6.6 Summary

There are probably other types of transitions that have not yet been identified and defined. However, the seduction, limbo and overlap transitions I have defined and described here are particularly useful and in therapy work they are worth remembering, both in the practice of therapy and also in the process of analysing what is going on in therapy sessions. Quite often when working therapeutically with clients, we don't think in a systematic and structured way that requires us specifically to do this or that, or pre-plan the introduction of a certain type of music followed by a transition to something else. Therapy, by its nature, is a spontaneously creative and dynamic process where the client and therapist are responding to each other, sometimes at quite an unconscious and intuitive level. Consequently, it is when one looks back on what has happened and becomes aware of it, that the occurrence of transitions becomes apparant. A part of us should stand back a bit from what's going on in the therapy session, thinking 'You're going round in circles…!', or 'Why not leave a space for something new to happen?'. The 'objective supervisor' concept of a part of us watching what's happening in therapy is very important as a monitor of our own reactions to clients, and an awareness of what's happening. This is particularly helpful when exploring the potential for transitions and the need for openness and flexibility to allow them to happen.

Finally, the flexibility and adaptability of the therapist musically is absolutely essential when undertaking frameworking or transitional processes. One could argue that there are a number of occasions when it's the therapist who needs to find a way of making a transition, even more than the client!

CHAPTER 7

Thematic Improvisation

Introduction

When we first begin working with a client in improvisational music making and we offer them the possibility to choose and use instruments, the sounds they make on the instruments they choose frequently form the starting point for building a musical interaction which leads to a musical relationship. Those sounds, sometimes coming in phrases, melodic contours or rhythmic patterns, are 'themes' or 'leitmotifs' which are the material with which we begin our musical engagement.

This chapter looks specifically at how a music therapist can respond to, support, extend and complement these themes by the use of a process of thematic improvisation. To begin with, the exercises in this chapter will concentrate on how to respond in a creative way at a mainly musical level, analysing and understanding the content of a theme, its different parts and its potential as a piece of musical material that can be adapted within the shared music making that goes on between the therapist and the client. Subsequently, the methods and techniques already described above will be reintroduced in order to build on the musical experience of developing thematic improvisation and give it a therapeutic direction.

A theme could be an idea, a concept, a mood or emotion, something that is either concrete or abstract. As well as the purely musical concept of a theme, this chapter will also address other forms of thematic improvisation.

7.1 The concept of 'theme' or 'leitmotif'

Let's start with the idea that clients produce short themes on a melody instrument. Figure 7.1 below gives some examples of different themes. They are short and I have written them specifically without any assigned meter, or marks for dynamics or tempo, in order that there should be no preconceived idea of how the theme should be accented or played. These themes have different parts to them that can provide the raw material for building a creative improvisation. The therapist is able to explore, in a musically creative way, different elements of the theme in order to develop a musical interaction or relationship that might address needs and issues with which the client may be working. There are various parts of the theme that can be independently used in a thematic improvisation. As it might not be clear whether the client has chosen to create a theme with a particular intention in mind, it is up to the therapist to explore all the various aspects of a musical theme in order to offer the client a creative way by which he or she can develop the musical engagement. Conversely, it may be that the client (given the necessary support) selects and works with a particular aspect of the theme.

Figure 7.1: Examples of themes

I will use Theme 1 from the list in Figure 7.1 to illustrate with examples on the CD just how much creative potential there is in a simple theme. For example, both the rhythm of this little theme and small sections of it, can be used in isolation without playing the melody line at all. Using the first four notes in the example, I have chosen to employ the same thematic rhythmic pattern as Beethoven used in the opening movement of the Fifth Symphony, from which he built a very substantial thematic improvisation, then re-introducing this theme in the third movement in a different form.

The following guidelines can be used to follow a number of different creative musical strategies in working with this theme. Each idea is demonstrated with an example on the CD.

- The melody line of this theme can be used alone, taking away the rhythm. It's a series of ascending phrases, and can be treated as a 4-note improvisation (see 3.1).

CD Example 55: Thematic improvisation using melody

- The harmony built into this theme can be used. As one can see, there is a feeling tonic-dominant-tonic in this theme going from G minor to D. The key of D doesn't indicate either major or minor, which leaves greater flexibility. There is also a feeling of B♭ major as well as D minor and D which can be used as the relative major to G minor.

CD Example 56: Thematic improvisation using harmony

- Tonal interval: a small section of the melody, for example the first two intervals, could be used for an interval-based improvisation on perfect 4ths and perfect 5ths. In CD57 it is demonstrated with a staccato style of playing.

CD Example 57: Thematic improvisation using tonal intervals

- Atonal interval: the last section of the theme contains a minor 2nd interval which could be used for an improvisation on its own, or the G, A, B♭ of the melody line can develop an atonal improvisation.

CD Example 58: Thematic improvisation using atonal intervals and style

- Ostinato figure/with melody: part of the theme, for example the first two intervals (DGA) could be used to create an ostinato figure in the bass, while the melody is freely improvised tonally, here using the 6ths and 3rds idea (see 3.8).

CD Example 59: Thematic improvisation using melody of theme as ostinato

- Grounding: the 5th interval which is part of the middle phrase of the theme could be used to give a ground to a melodic improvisation above. This can give a Celtic feel to the music (see 3.10).

CD Example 60: Thematic improvisation using interval of the theme as a ground

- Melodic contour: Ignoring the precise notes of the melody, the mere contour of it can be used to give a sensation of ascending melodic phrases.

CD Example 61: Thematic improvisation using only the contour of the melody

- Placing the theme in inversion, one can create a falling melodic phrase such as B-A-G-D to give an ostinato in the right hand while the left hand plays a different melody. In CD62 the B♭ is changed to a B natural to give the major (bright) feeling.

CD Example 62: thematic improvisation using melody in inversion, left hand tune

- Meter: the original theme doesn't specify a meter and also has a pause at the end of the first two phrases. By specifying a meter (for example 3/4 or 4/4) one can create a sense of ground pulse and part ground rhythm.

CD Example 63: Thematic improvisation using theme and varying meter

Clinical application

In clinical work the use of thematic improvisation involves not only using elements from the theme, but also developing other musical ideas to build up the potential of the music (and the therapy process) that requires both therapist and client to 'move on' from the original thematic material. The theme, or parts of it, act as a foundation to which either therapist or client can return, and may help the client to move away from stuck or resistant positions. Both client and therapist can become blocked by being stuck in repetitive musical patterns, therefore it would be helpful in the process of developing thematic improvisation to specify some 'don'ts'.

Table 7.1 The Don'ts!

- *Don't* get stuck on playing the whole theme.
- *Don't* get stuck in the key in which the theme is written (in this case, G minor).
- *Don't* get stuck on one rhythmic element from the theme.
- *Don't* forget the importance of variability in tempo.
- *Don't* forget the importance of variability in volume.
- *Don't* get stuck in 'piano style' playing (left hand octaves, right hand melody).

There are ways to overcome these 'don'ts' and, in particular, most improvisers need to allow themselves on occasions some 'thinking time', in order to be able to get out of a repetitive pattern of playing, or think of a new direction in which to go. This 'thinking time' was discussed in 6.3.

7.2 Rhythmic thematic improvisation

Rhythm and tempo provide an important focus in clinical improvisation. The rhythm of the theme can be used for an improvisation, where the other elements of the theme can be discarded (melody, harmony, etc.). An element in the theme could be used as a ground 'ostinato' rhythm, and this is often a useful strategy where it's important to provide a stable foundation for improvisation. It helps particularly with clients who lack stability in their playing and have a therapeutic need for a secure framework.

Figure 7.2 gives another selection of short themes, also without any bar lines to indicate meter or dynamic markings. I have taken these examples from experiences in clinical work where clients tend to create themes in a variety of ways on either piano or melodic instruments such as vibraphones and xylophones. Some analysis of how this occurs has revealed the following methods, which I have correlated where possible with the examples in Figure 7.2:

- random – no intention to try to create a musical theme (theme 1);
- song-based – trying to pick out a familiar melody (themes 2 and 7);
- musical – spontaneously creating a tonal melody with an underlying pulse (themes 3 and 6);
- chaotic – jumping from one idea to another (themes 1 and 4);
- circular – creating a theme that is rather stuck and seems to go round in circles (theme 5);
- step-wise – going up and down one note at a time (theme 6);
- playful – with surprises and exaggerations (theme 7);
- motoric – the pattern of movement in the body creates the music.

The theme can be partitioned to use different rhythmic sub-figures or part-figures. The process involves varying tempo, stretching out the rhythm, and interspersing the rhythmic patterns with other material. There are many different ways in which rhythmic improvisation using the rhythm of the theme can be accomplished, both with and without an underlying pulse. In fact, it is quite important to be able to improvise freely without pulse as well as to establish and use a pulse

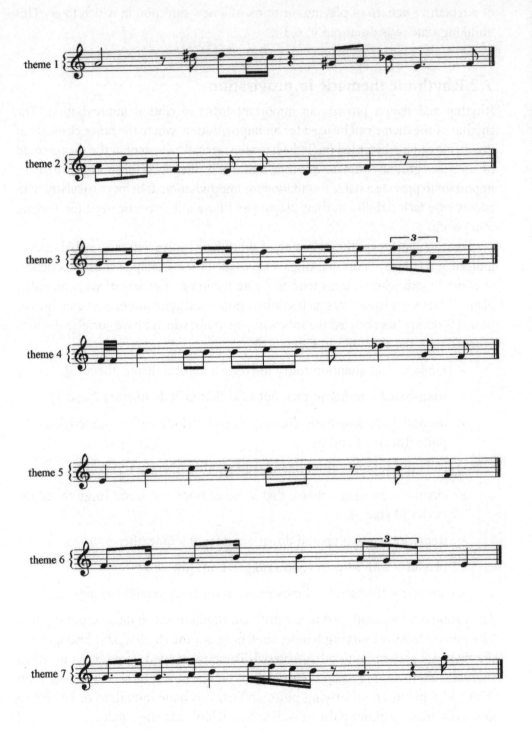

Figure 7.2: Examples of thematic production in clients

CD64 demonstrates in a short space a variety of ways in which the rhythmic elements from a theme can change and vary. I will use the rhythmic idea inbuilt in theme 3 of Figure 7.2 (GGC GGD GGE ECAF) to show how one can begin and develop a rhythmic improvisation, firstly starting on the piano, then transferring to the drum.

CD Example 64: Thematic improvisation using the rhythmic elements of a theme

Important potentials when trying to develop rhythmic improvisation are:

- improvising using a rhythmic figure, but without pulse;
- improvising with the same rhythmic figure using a pulse;
- rhythmic dialogues – where a rhythmic theme is used to build a dialogue between two players;
- establishing a pulse but without imposing a meter on it where random accents can disrupt any sense of meter;
- establishing a steady pulse with a meter where the accents can accentuate the meter;
- establishing a pulse with a meter that can change (4/4, 2/3/4 or 7/8–8/8 (8/8 being with a Latin American 3+3+2 style).

Exercise: Use the rhythm of the themes in Figure 7.2 on a drum rather than the piano, improvising in the ways described above.

7.3 Melodic thematic improvisation

Melody, in particular the phrases that occur in melodic sequences, can be construed as a metaphor for sentences and the intervals and direction of that melody also act as a metaphor for the inflexions of speech. Therefore melody, especially in melodic dialogue, can sound remarkably like two people talking together (or even arguing together!) as I have discussed earlier (3.4, 3.7 and 4.5). The way in which clients spontaneously produce melody is also particularly interesting. In my clinical area, I have noted that clients (especially autistic clients) often produce repetitive melody patterns and, when they are insecure or perhaps somewhat uncreative, their melodies may also be rather limited in range and proceed in a step-wise fashion. I also find that clients who have a lack of structure and direction in what they are doing can create melodies that represent this as a wandering line that doesn't seem to go anywhere, with a lack of repetition or spontaneously developed melodic form.

Using the melody of the themes is therefore a powerful option, while varying and sometimes excluding other elements of it, particularly sometimes the rhythm patterns and underlying tempo. Note-lengths in the theme can also be varied in order to change the sense of rhythm that may have been present in its initial form.

Here is another set of themes for use in developing melodic thematic improvisation. Again, the objective is the same – to use all or different parts of the theme to expand and develop the melody in the context of an improvisation.

Figure 7.3: Examples of themes for melodic development

I have deliberately chosen a theme that is chromatic (Theme 1 from Figure 7.3), to try to demonstrate the potentials with dissonant and atonal melodic improvisation. The example in Figure 7.4 begins with the theme (bar 1), then establishes a melody dialogue between right and left hand, where the left hand also uses elements of the theme (bars 2–8). The tritone in the theme is then used (bars 9–12), following which a new idea develops with a sequential use of the rising 4th figure (bars 13–15). A harmonic development takes place, initially using the 5th in the opening of the theme (bars 16–18) and then developing with the tritone again (19–22). At bar 23, the left hand accompanies while the right hand uses the melodic contour of the theme (23–32), after which chords (mainly 2nd inversions – see 3.8) use the step-wise 2nds in the theme together with the 4th interval jump (bars 32–37). After bar 37, the chromatic ideas in the theme are there, together with the interval jumps,

Figure 7.4: Melodic improvisation, continued on next page

Figure 7.4: Melodic improvisation, continued

but the improvisation has actually transcended to a different level, where the original theme is present more as a memory, a set of musical ideas.

In CD65, I convert the theme using the melodic contour to show how you can extend the idea into more diatonic and tonal improvisation, as well as using the pentatonic scale. The example uses other techniques such as sequences, melody dialogue, two chord improvisations, as well as therapeutic methods such as tonal grounding and accompanying ideas, in order to demonstrate how the ideas earlier in the book become integrated into thematic improvisation.

CD Example 65: Example of melodic thematic improvisation 1

A final example of melodic improvisation uses theme 3 from Figure 7.3, and demonstrates how much harmony is inherent in some melodies. In fact, many melodies (especially folk melodies) hold within them the underpinning harmonic structure of the tune (for example, 'Greensleeves', played in D minor includes the chords D minor, C major, A major and F major in the melodic line – coming as broken chords). CD66 demonstrates the way the harmony in the theme can be used, both in the melodic improvisation, and also where the notes of the theme form a harmonic ground.

CD Example 66: Example of melodic thematic improvisation 2

7.4 Thematic improvisation incorporating musical techniques and therapeutic methods

In clinical music therapy work, thematic ideas become integrated and rapid changes can occur in the musical material of the therapist and client. We don't typically set out to design a therapeutic approach for a client where they are instructed to play in a certain way. The ideas documented previously were designed as exercises for a person to develop his or her improvisational techniques. In the last few examples I have begun to connect together these different techniques in order to apply them as methods in clinical situations.

The next selection of exercises involves combining the material from specific themes (or parts of themes) using some of the musical techniques and therapeutic methods that have been explained in earlier chapters. The options that can be employed using the theme, both as a whole and in its various musical parts, are potentially infinite. In the next three figures, I have notated three different musical fragments (themes), representing the kind of material a client may initiate in an improvisation. Figure 7.5 is a melody (using material from theme 4 in Figure 7.3), containing rhythm, a meter, and some implied harmony. The notated example provides some ideas for developing a melodic, thematic improvisation.

Figure 7.6 is a chordal theme, founded in the pentatonic scale. Again, the notated example provides some ideas of different ways in which the theme (first 3 bars) can be developed. This can be used as a starting point for a chordal thematic improvisation in the pentatonic mode.

Figure 7.7 is a purely rhythmic theme, but assuming the use of bongos, therefore placed on to different tones, an upper and a lower. Again, the example provides the foundation and ideas for an exercise in rhythmic thematic improvisation.

The objective here is to incorporate and integrate in a flowing process many of the techniques and methods described above, using necessary transitions to allow change to occur in the musical improvisation. In order to provide some inspiration and examples of what I mean, I have formulated some suggested sequences below – purely for practice purposes – to provide different frameworks with which to experiment. The sequences imply a therapeutic process that may involve development, regression or a static state. This is often the reality in therapy work, and the significance of transitions should not be underestimated in order to allow a variety of emotional processes and interpersonal communications (both ways!) to emerge in the musical material including:

> I'm lost…
>
> I don't know what's happening…
>
> I don't like this…
>
> I want to try this…
>
> That's good…
>
> I'm not listening…
>
> Please help me…
>
> Etcetera, etcetera!

These exercises include certain parameters that one can follow, but don't forget that there is a range of musical parameters which should always be attended to or varied as appropriate. I am talking particularly about volume, tempo, duration of sound and spaces in the music. The need for spaces and silence in the music is also significantly important and worthy of a separate section.

Figure 7.5: Melody with rhythm, meter and inherent harmony

Figure 7.6: Chordal and pentatonic

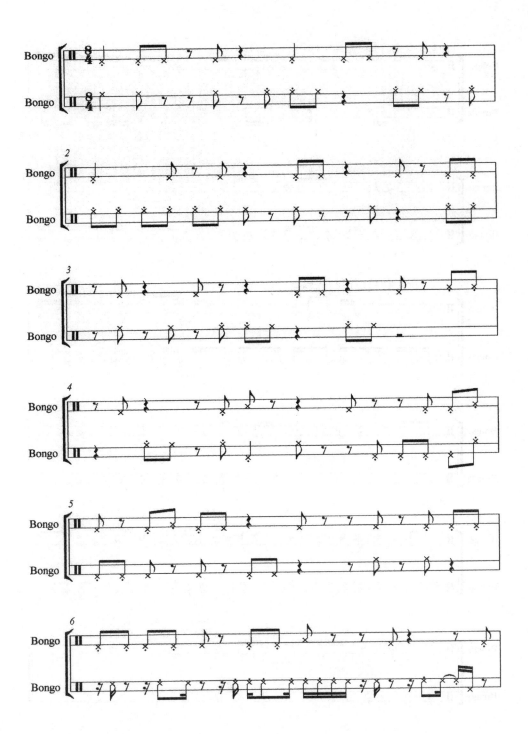

Figure 7.7: Rhythmic theme – bongos, continued on next page

Figure 7.7: Rhythmic theme – bongos, continued

Table 7.2 Practice examples for musical and therapeutic process in improvisation

Process 1

Individual	Starts theme	Develops rhythmic idea	Transition: loses pulse	Plays with melody	Transition	Starts using rhythm alone

Process 2 (2 people)

Client	Starts theme	Gets stuck	Reacts – chaotic music	Limbo transition	Rhythmic patterns	Gets lost
Therapist	Accompanies	Overlaps transition	Grounding and containing	Introduces structure – tonal frame	Matching	Reflecting

Process 3 (2 people)

Client	Starts theme	Transition	Dialogue	Gets stuck	Inspired	Transition
Therapist	Matches	Transition	Dialogue	Framework	Accompanies	Transition to end

Space in the music

There are a number of reasons why there should be spaces in improvised music making. Music needs to be understood as a combination of sounds and silence, and the silence is just as important an element when creating an effect in spontaneously improvised music as sound. In fact, the sounds will have more impact when emerging from pauses or periods of silence. In clinical work, there are some compelling reasons why therapists should leave spaces in the music:

- to allow some silence to occur during music making
- to have a space of silence before starting to play and when finishing playing
- to allow for some 'thinking time' during which a new idea may occur
- to stop music that has become repetitive and uncreative
- to have time to listen and reflect on the sounds that are being made

- to allow space for a client to change the direction of the style of music that is going on

- to allow space for the therapist to change the direction of the style of music that is going on.

Consequently, the 'spaces' in the music may be silence, or may be where the musical 'flow' has halted:

1. pausing on a note or on a chord, sustaining the sound with the pedal;

2. stopping playing and allowing silence to occur;

3. when playing in a rhythmical pattern with an underlying pulse, creating 'silence' spaces where the pulse (sound) is implied for a jazzy or syncopated effect.

7.5 Conclusion

The exercises presented in this chapter assist in putting together the musical and therapeutic methods that have been described above which are the building blocks of successful and creative improvisation. In the advanced clinical keyboard improvisation courses at Aalborg University, the teaching of which has supplied much of the inspiration for this book, the students are required to make a five-minute, thematic improvisation on the piano as part of the final exam. They are also required to make a three-part improvisation on themes drawn from a picture (using transitions between parts), and improvise as a duet with an examiner playing on drums, xylophones and other instruments (using both musical techniques and therapeutic methods). Compared with the other two elements, thematic improvisation often provokes the most anxiety. It really is creating music based on a musical idea (the students are given short themes to use similar to those in Figures 7.1, 7.3, and 7.4), and tests the capacity to build up a musical creation in a spontaneous way. For composers and musicians, this process can involve playing in a familiar style, and using the techniques and musical ideas with which one feels most comfortable – whether it is in the style of a Bach two-part invention, or a structured, twentieth-century jazz idiom. For the music therapist, the style has to align closely with the musical expression, potentials and limitations of a client, or group of clients. In reality, there will be a multitude of other factors to take into consideration, from the influence of the pathology to the mood on a particular day. The development of a musical relationship through music based on an idea or 'theme' presented by the client relies on the therapist's skill in both nurturing as well as exploiting musical material produced by the client.

A theme can be like an identity, a 'signature tune', a facial expression, or an emotional reaction. Musical themes have structure, implications, meaning, and when they come up consistently in the playing together of two people, they also become part of the musical language that builds up, underpinning a shared musical understanding that connects and intensifies the relationship. Themes and melodies have even been used as codes, which perhaps shouldn't surprise us. Two examples that spring to mind are the famous opening statement of the first movement of Beethoven's Fifth Symphony (used by the BBC in broadcasts during World War II because the rhythm spelt out the Morse Code for the letter V), and a completely unknown but delightful melody that contained a coded message that Michael Redgrave valiantly tried to remember in the 1938 film *The Lady Vanishes*.

This chapter has tried to provide a way of understanding the process of thematic improvisation. It is not a precise art, but there are many skills involved. The acquisition and development of techniques does, as usual, hold the key to achieving more fluency and fluidity in thematic improvisation. People may be anxious about this method because it requires the most effort in cognitive thinking, drawing on analysis and structure as skills to make a satisfying musical creation. Sometimes I think of it in the same way as creative cookery – it is not the amount or number of different ingredients that you have at your disposal, or even the importance of a complex recipe, it is what you do with the material that counts. In therapy work, I consider the client's musical play, their 'theme', as the potential manifestation of many aspects or characteristics of their personality. My music, in response to that idea, is my musical reaction to their musical personality. The development of our thematic improvisation is, in a metaphoric way, the development of our musical and personal relationship, and that relationship will be determined by the potentials and skills I can utilize in thematic improvisation.

CHAPTER 8

Group Improvisation

Some of the ideas documented in this chapter were specifically developed in work involving group improvisation. The work that I am describing is drawn from group therapy sessions I had over many years with clients in a large hospital for people with moderate to severe learning disability. Consequently these ideas may or may not be appropriate for clients from other pathological populations. However, I believe that they are generalizable and, as such, quite usable. It depends on the degree of concreteness and also the underpinning therapeutic philosophy as to whether or not they can be adapted for use with other populations.

Nevertheless, the ideas described here, and in the preceding chapters, are not intended to be used as fixed or standardized procedures. It would not be to the advantage of music therapy to become 'manualized' – where a defined (and rigid) procedure was followed in treatment situations. This would actually reduce one of the main strengths of music therapy – its flexibility and adaptability to the clients' needs. However, while we develop a knowledge base in theory, and a skill base in music, there needs to be a potential field of activity, using tried and tested methods and techniques that can be drawn on and applied. The application of these methods and techniques relies more on defining the healthcare needs of clients, and conse-quently the objectives or direction of therapy, than on a treatment 'manual'.

I have taught a systematic procedure for understanding the function of therapy, and therefore the choice (or intuitive use) of interventions, based on the following process:

- Gain knowledge of the history of the client.
- Gain knowledge of the pathology/personality of the client.

- Define the primary healthcare /educational needs of the client from the point of view of the *therapist.*

- Define the primary healthcare/educational needs of the client from the point of view of the *client.*

- Undertake an assessment to confirm these needs, and evaluate music therapy as an indicated treatment in meeting them.

- Define the objectives or general direction of the therapy based on those needs.

- Decide the methods and techniques that are most likely to be helpful in facilitating therapy.

- Decide how to baseline/record/evaluate these methods.

- Evaluate the efficacy of the methods and adjust interventions accordingly.

Therefore in discussing 'methods and techniques' – whether to use verbal interventions or not, whether to use receptive or active techniques, be directive or non-directive, structured or non-structured, use songs, improvisation, tonal or atonal – there are implications that decisions that need to be grounded in the procedure I describe above, and related to client needs (Wigram 1995b, 1996a, 1996b).

The potential intervention techniques using improvisation are described in the 'menu' of therapeutic thematic improvisation ideas in Table 8.2. But to start with it is interesting to explore how one builds up a music making experience in a group and to do that, we often use warming-up methods with the group that are not specifically designed to have a deep therapeutic focus, but are rather experiences by which we can engage clients in group music making.

This chapter provides many different ideas for musical (and movement) techniques, and therapeutic methods for use in group improvisation. It is structured in a way that follows some of the potential structure of a group music therapy session. I begin by describing a number of different warm-up techniques I have used, some of which can also be applied as therapeutic methods. The chapter then develops more ideas based on thematic improvisation, or improvisations that are framed or supported by play rules. I also discuss the potential for structure and freedom in the play rules that are used in group work, relating to therapeutic methods, and the idea of concrete, abstract or emotional themes on which play rules can be based. Finally, the value and structure of different musical forms is discussed, followed by a concluding section (not entirely specific to group work) on the influence of transference and counter-transference.

8.1 Warm-up techniques

I have used a number of warm-up techniques over the years and am including a short selection of them here, together with their therapeutic value. The warm-ups can be musically active, musically receptive, vocal, and involve movement or relaxation exercises. There are many different types and one tends to build up an appropriate repertoire that is relevant to the clients with whom one is working.

Each warm-up described has play rules attached to it which indicate how to introduce it to a typical group of clients. Characteristically, warm-ups have a fairly clear structure, even if they contain hidden potentials. They are designed and used for 'breaking the ice' or preparation for a therapy, and from them may often come the themes and issues that will underpin or focus towards more intensive and deeper therapeutic experiences. They are intended to have their own therapeutic goals, and there are many therapeutic benefits to be gained from quite simple and non-threatening warm-ups. For example, they can often be used to reduce potential anxieties in individual clients or groups either about music therapy as a process, or even about being in therapy. Most of the warm-ups described below can be used in group, or in individual work.

Familiarity and confidence

At this point, I would like to make a comment regarding the expectations we may have of our clients, and their potentials in active, improvisational music making. Let us try to remember that as music therapists, we have all been trained to play and to improvise, and feel familiar and comfortable with instruments. Also, if vocal training and vocal improvisation has been included in our training, we will also be confident to use our voices. The great majority of our clients, on the other hand, have not trained in improvisation, and many may never have learnt an instrument, sung in a choir, and will tell you that they are 'not musical'. Even if they have had a musical education, they may feel uncomfortable to be required to create music spontaneously through improvisation, and need to be led into the process with a degree of care and sensitivity. It is not appropriate to describe a client's lack of response or limited musical production as 'resistance' or 'demonstrating psychological blocks' when they may actually feel inadequate or uncomfortable with using instruments at all, particularly using them for free improvisation. The warm-ups that I describe are used for overcoming these types of difficulty, and for explaining, modelling and then rehearsing with clients how they can use instruments or their voice, introducing them, in this way, to the fundamental tenet of improvisational music therapy that we can express ourselves through improvised music making sometimes more effectively than with verbal language.

Table 8.1 Warm-up techniques

Instrumental	Vocal	Relaxation, preparation or movement
Explore the sound	Group humming	Relaxation induction
Pass a message	Welcome songs	Preparation exercises – being present
Musical portrait of yourself	The echo game with voices	Rhythmic movement warm-up
Musical portrait of your ideal self	Start one at a time (vocal)	Melodic movement warm-up
Musical portrait of another	The 'conducting' game	Song and movement warm-up
The 'echo' game	Soft – loud – soft (vocal)	
Start one at a time		
The 'conducting' game		
Soft – loud – soft		

The instruments in the room may be placed in the middle of a circle of clients or could be placed around the room or on shelves or in cupboards. The issue of where the instruments are again depends on the client population.

1. *Explore the sound*: Explain to the clients that you would like them each to choose an instrument that they would like to 'explore' or 'try out' and invite them to make a few sounds on their chosen instrument to see what sort of noises it can produce. It can be useful to model this first, showing how to explore the instrument creatively, avoid creating a musical structure, and establish a time frame. After each member of the group has explored his or her instrument, the therapist can ask them if they liked their instrument, and perhaps even if they disliked another's. Avoid asking the clients to 'play how you feel', because perhaps merely by asking them they will be careful to disguise how they feel, or avoid playing altogether!

Therapeutic value:

- The choice of instrument can be revealing.
- The way of playing can represent aspects of personality and character.
- The way of playing can represent aspects of musical history, preference, and cultural background.
- The way of playing can represent the influence of pathology.
- The way of playing and body language or posture can represent mood, intentionality, communicability, expressivity, awareness, perception, and motor coordination.

In fact, using this simple play rule of 'explore the instrument, see what it sounds like', will result in the client revealing something of how they feel, without it being a demand (or a pressure).

2. *Send a message:* Explain to the clients that you would like them each to choose an instrument that they like the look of. Then explain that this warm-up experience involves sending a musical message to someone else in the group. One person will start, choosing a person in the group to whom they would like to send a message, and saying their name. The person to whom the message is sent should just listen and 'receive' the message, without having to respond. Then they can choose someone in the group to whom they would like to send a new message – their own message. It can also be useful to model this exercise first, so that members of the group can understand that the message lies within the dynamic and quality of the sounds that are made, rather than in a particular musical style or structure.

    Therapeutic value:

- All those listed under the first warm-up 'explore the sound' also apply here.
- Group dynamics emerge – who chooses to send a message to whom, how the message is received, and what the attitude is of the other group members.
- The quality and style of the message can be relevant for interpretation.
- For the clients it is a good experience to give, or do, something for another.

- For the clients it is also a good experience to be given something – to receive.

- The musical production doesn't only represent the client, it can also represent the client's attitude to another.

- Emotions begin to become more significant – humour, sarcasm, friendliness or hostility.

    It would be wise to point out that in spite of my enthusiasm for seeing the therapeutic potential of warm-ups, I would also exercise caution at over-interpreting the experience and the clients' behaviour.

3. *Make a musical portrait of yourself as you are now*: Invite the clients to choose one or more instruments and try to use them to make some sounds that could represent a musical portrait of them as they are now. This can be varied to be a representation of themselves as they are in this phase of their treatment, or in this week, month, year, or in this phase of their life. It would be wise not to model this, as that could be construed by the client as suggestive of how they should represent themselves. It might be wise to put a time limit. You can ask for feedback, or make an observation after each client, or wait until everyone in the group that wants to has done it. Or, you can avoid asking or expecting the client (or yourself) to offer verbal explanation or comment, and leave it entirely as a musical experience. These decisions are down to client need and therapeutic judgement.

4. *Make a musical portrait of yourself as you would like to be – your ideal self.* Invite the clients to choose one or more instruments and try to use them to make some sounds that could represent a musical portrait of their ambitions about their ideal self. Give the play rule that asks the client to imagine all the characteristics and attributes they would like to have – imagining being their ideal person – and then play it. Here, we can try to move the client closer to actually playing an image or experience, rather than producing 'sound effects' that represent something, but are more objective. Both this experience and the last can be subjective.

    Therapeutic value for warm-ups 3 and 4:

- This time, the sounds on the instrument are directly representing the client.

- Look for congruence between how the client presents verbally, and then musically.

- It is sometimes easier to play yourself than to try to explain yourself.

- There are some thing things you can express musically that you can't express verbally.

- Used over time, in both these warm-ups the way of presenting oneself (or one's ideal self) musically may change – informing both therapist and client about the client's perception of him or herself.

5.   *Make a musical portrait of another person in the group*: Invite the clients to choose one or more instruments and try to use them to make some sounds that could represent a musical portrait of another in the group. They must identify whom it is they are 'painting' musically. This warm-up has obvious risks. The musical portraits could be empathic, and reveal insight and care from one client towards another. They could also be challenging, provoking, perhaps even insulting, and the consequences could be negative reactions within the group.

   Therapeutic value:

- The sounds on the instrument directly represent the client's perception of another.

- This may promote and develop group dynamics and build up understanding within the group.

- It is sometimes easier to play a feeling or something you would like to explain to another than to say it verbally.

- There are some things you can express musically that you can't express verbally.

- It is a (risky) way for someone to become aware of his or her effect on others.

6.   *The 'echo' game: instrumental*: The play rule is that everyone finds an instrument they would like to use. One person starts, and makes a sound or plays a short phrase on his instrument. He is the leader. Everyone else then plays that exact sound or phrase back to the leader (like an echo) – *all at the same time*, trying to match the dynamics, quality and style of the leader's sound. The leader continues to make sounds and phrases, each time waiting for the group to 'echo' his sound. It is useful to model this, and to demonstrate that as well as playing short themes or rhythms in a musical way, you can make unusual, perhaps even funny sounds. When the volunteer leader has had enough of being 'echoed', or at a sign from

the group therapist, they then nominate another person in the group to be leader. There may be people in the group who don't want to be the 'leader' – or have to deal with that level of attention on them. There may also be people in the group who love being 'in the spotlight', and want to be leader a lot, and for a long time. The therapist needs to take care of both clients. This is a great warm-up with certain groups, for example, children and people with learning disability.

7. *The 'echo' game: vocal:* This warm-up is really quite similar to the previous one, but using the voice rather than instruments. The play rules are the same, and with some groups it can help to start with an instrument, and then take it into using the voice. People can be quite cautious about improvising with their voice. It is a very personal form of expression, and people can be embarrassed about sounds they make. It would also help to model this, and maybe to encourage unusual vocal sounds to draw the group away from assuming it should a sung rhythm or phrase (musical style production). For example, a cough, snigger, shout, animal sound, different types of laugh, clucking, lip or mouth sounds, for example, can all be introduced in this warm-up.

    Therapeutic value:

    - It develops listening processes, and giving attention to someone.

    - It develops turn-taking, and empathic playing ability and sensitivity to others.

    - For the leader – it provides a feeling of control and power.

    - For the followers, it gives the satisfaction of just having to imitate someone and feel part of a group doing it – therefore it engenders group feeling.

    - Enjoyment – fun and humour can come into this warm-up.

    - It shows how some leaders may seek to find new, unusual even crazy sound, while other leaders are happy to copy or follow ideas from other group members.

    - All the therapeutic benefits from the first warm-up also apply.

8. *Begin playing, or making vocal sounds, in turn – and then stop in turn:* The play rules start when the therapist invites the clients to choose an instrument or use their voice. Then explain that the play rule is that one person will start, and then each other group member will join in one at a time –

allowing a period each time before they start, until everyone is playing/vocalizing. Then after some time of the whole group playing/vocalizing, the first person to start will stop, followed in turn by everyone, until only the last person to join is left playing on his own.

9. *The 'conducting' game*: The play rule is that one person in the group takes the role of 'conductor', and places herself in the middle of the circle. She can use a drumbeater – or simply her hand. She is not going to beat time – it's not that type of conducting. She is going to point at a client when she wants them to start playing, and put up an open hand 'stop' sign when she wants them to stop. Get louder and softer can be indicated by waving arms upwards (palm uppermost), and pushing hands down (palm side down). Faster and slower can also have their own signs. The idea of this warm-up is to allow someone to create his or her own music and texture, bringing in and then stopping group members from playing, and creating dyads and triads in the group. In a group of six clients, anywhere between one and six people will be playing at any one time. The conductor is not telling them *how or what* to play – just when. It works best if the conductor withdraws (hides) a little, getting physically out if the way to let the musical interactions develop that he/she has initiated and facilitated.

    Therapeutic value:

    - Listening to each other.

    - Working on a group 'task' that involves cooperating.

    - Facilitating (or provoking) a group member to take a key role.

    - The conducting game allows exploration of group dynamics and group relationships.

    - Both warm-ups 9 and 10 facilitate a group learning about not playing all the time. It is a weakness of group improvisation that there seems to be a driving motivation to play all the time. These break down that pattern.

    - Both warm-ups 9 and 10 vary the texture, quality and style of the improvisation.

10. *Soft – loud – soft*: The first play rule is that this warm-up can be done with instruments or with voices. The idea is that everyone can start playing/vocalizing together, whatever they like, but very softly. Then

gradually, working together to achieve this, the group gets louder, to an agreed intensity (i.e. *f*, *ff* or *fff*). After a short period of loud playing/vocalizing, the group starts to get softer quite gradually until they have gone back to playing very softly. It is important in this warm-up to check the tolerance of individuals in the group to loud volume, and contain excessively loud clients, otherwise it might serve the opposite purpose from that intended!

Therapeutic value:

- As in warm-ups 8 and 9, this calls for group cooperation, and a level of individual control to follow and be together with the rest of the group.

- It also promotes the feeling that everyone in the group is *part of a whole*. Rather than engaging in interactive, communicative improvising, which is more evident in warm-ups 1–6, this warm-up (as in 7–9) is a collaboration in the group all to create something together. The outcome is a group musical product.

- It reveals how well people can work with loudness and softness, and who in the group has difficulties in this area.

11. *Group humming*: The play rule is that each member of the group finds a note at a pitch that they feel comfortable with and starts to hum, holding the sound for as long as possible before breathing and starting to hum the note again. It is often a good idea to ask group members to close their eyes for this experience. Sitting, standing or lying is also optional, depending on the clients. The result is the sound of a group all humming different notes. The sound can also be varied, from humming to 'Aaahhh-ing' to 'Zzzzzzzzzzzz-ing', etc.

Therapeutic value:

- It is an easy warm-up and can be used with most groups.

- Clients feel centred on their own sound, and start to listen to themselves.

- Clients feel they are part of a whole group vocal sound.

- Sometimes soloists emerge, singing more loudly or with a different timbre from others.

- It provides the possibility to make a vocal expression without any judgement about skill or 'niceness' of your sound.

12. *Welcome songs (and farewell songs)*: This is a common activity with both individuals and groups, and is a frequently appropriate way to begin a session as a warm-up. Many have been composed, and everyone has their favourites. They can be sung straight – in tempo, and in a meter, or they can be sung flexibly (I often recommend this), pausing at certain points in the song to allow the client(s) to respond vocally/verbally, or make a sound on an instrument. Creativity and variability is also essential in the presentation of both welcome and farewell songs when sung to individuals. There needs to be a matching and congruence in the style and quality of presentation related to the individual to whom it is being sung.

Therapeutic value:

- It provides clear boundaries to the beginning and end of a session.
- It engages members of the group individually.
- Group members feel recognized.
- It is possible to adjust the quality and presentation style to individuals.
- Familiarity, which provides security.
- It is a communicative activity.

13. *Relaxation induction*: This is a warm-up, or a form of preparation for a particular type of therapy experience, such as Guided Imagery and Music (GIM). Typically, the therapist will ask the individual or group to find a space to be comfortable, sitting or lying, and then ask them to close their eyes and follow the suggestions of the therapist. Sometimes mats, pillows and rugs are used. When asking people to lie on a thin mat on the floor, remember to offer them a pillow or cushion both for under their head and for under their knees, as the pressure on the spine when lying completely flat can work against the relaxation hoped for. Relaxation inductions can be more directed towards psychological relaxation, such as asking clients to clear their mind, find a focus place where they feel very safe and comfortable, or be directed towards physical relaxation, working through the body from bottom to top or vice versa, and gradually spacing out the instructions, and getting softer with shorter sentences. There is also a method involving tension and relaxation, where the therapist will ask clients to increase the tension in the muscles of their arms, for example, hold their breath, and then after three to six

seconds ask them to relax the muscles, and slowly let out their breath. The therapeutic value of these warm-ups is self-evident.

Therapeutic value:

- It creates a certain therapeutic atmosphere.
- It reduces tension and anxiety.
- It creates open feelings, and openness to the experiences to come.
- It helps clients (and therapists) feel present in the environment.
- It promotes a feeling of physical comfort.

14. *Preparation exercises – being present:* This is a warm-up that may involve neither music nor movement, or could involve both. It is the most flexible style of warm-up, and is intended to try to help an individual client, or group of clients, settle down, attend to where they are, and feel 'present' in the therapy space and open to the experiences they will be having. Therefore there are many different ways this can be done: sitting quietly with closed eyes and listening to the sounds around, and the sounds of each other being alive (breathing, etc.); standing up, finding a free space in the room where you can spread your arms out without touching others, and then going through a series of grounding and orienting movements; feeling the ground beneath your feet, bending your knees and then straightening, turning your body to each side while keeping your feet fixed in one position, stretching up to 'touch the sky', and down to 'touch the earth'; breathing exercises – fast, slow, holding breath, panting, blowing, sighing.

15. *Rhythmic movement warm-up:* This warm-up can be done sitting or standing. The play rules involve movements that can be done to a rhythmic stimulus. That stimulus could be live music, a drum, vocal pattern, or it could be a CD or tape of rhythmic music. The movements can vary from rhythmic exercises with feet, arms and body movements to clapping, patting or stroking one's body rhythmically. The music definitely needs to be of a style and at a speed that can be managed by the particular clients with whom one is using this warm-up. Play rules can also involve suggesting to clients they pretend that they are machines, or that they are playing rhythm instruments, or that they are taking part in a rhythmic dance.

16. *Melodic movement warm-up*: This is significantly different from the
     rhythmic movements, and in fact should exclude pulse, in order to focus
     on a different type of movement. The idea is to work with movements
     that represent phrases, height and depth, and nuances in the melody. The
     music used could be live, or a CD, and should be non-pulsed. Play rules
     for this warm-up might involve moving one's arms in a style that reflects
     the melody, or suggesting to clients they can pretend they are a flower
     opening up, or that they are taking part in a ballet. As with the rhythmic
     movement exercise, there are many possibilities.

17. *Song and movement warm-up*: With some groups, clients need quite a
     concrete and structured movement experience, and 'action' songs can be
     a well-structured model. There are many different action songs, some
     that involve the clients fitting the actions into the rhythm or pattern of
     the song, such as 'Head and Shoulders, Knees and Toes', or others where
     there is a space in the lyrics and pulse/rhythm for the clients to make an
     action in their own time – such as 'If You're Happy and You Know it'.
     These songs are more typically used with children, or with children and
     adults with learning disability, but they are also applied in aged care
     (action songs will always retain an affection in the hearts of older adults
     in the UK since King George VI memorably led a group of servicemen
     and servicewomen in a rendition of 'Underneath the Spreading Chestnut
     Tree' during the war to lift morale!).

Therapeutic value of the movement warm-ups:

- to ground clients and help them to be aware of their bodies
- to encourage movement in clients who are rather stuck or static
- to be aware of the environment of the therapy room and their place in it
- to stimulate and raise the level of physical and psychological energy
- to lose inhibitions and break down barriers
- to promote motor coordination, and a feeling of physical power
- for the therapist to be able to see the physical behaviour of the clients.

These are only some examples of warm-ups in sessions – there are many more possibilities. They serve a purpose, and they have therapeutic intention and value. The
clients can often decide and show what helps them best. Some are more musically
structured, while others have an inter-personal or intra-personal function. Some are

clearly inappropriate for certain types of clients, or therapeutic situations. But after the opening welcome in a session, a warm-up acts as a form of transition or preparation for the therapy experiences to follow.

Characteristics of a therapy session

Therapy sessions have some logical and frequently consistent elements to them; in order for the clients to feel secure and safe there must be some degree of predictability in what is going to occur. In some models of music therapy, a very loose format is often employed which tends to include the following sequence of events. This is typically used with verbal clients.

1.   Opening – welcoming the client(s) to the therapy room (music or verbal discussion).

2.   Initialising the therapy (welcome songs or warm-ups).

3.   Finding the theme or issue (from what happened in a warm-up experience or through further discussion).

4.   Improvisational experiences relating to the theme.

5.   Discussion.

6.   Further improvisational experiences.

7.   Discussion

8.   Closure – ending the session.

The first part of this chapter has given examples of opening experiences and warm-up techniques. The next section goes on to suggest further frames and extensions to thematic improvisation, which can also employ the improvisational and musical techniques, therapeutic methods and transitional techniques described in Chapters 3, 4, 5 and 6.

8.2 Play rules, themes, media and structure – the foundations of improvisation

To meet the need for a range of play rules, structure or lack of structure in an improvisation, I have formulated a scheme of play rules with five different criteria (Table 8.2) upon which the improvisation may be constructed:

- thematic criteria
- structure of activity

- medium of music making

- style of music

- degree of directional control in the improvisation.

The function of play rules has been described previously, and they are also referred to by Bruscia as 'givens', in his method of Experimental Improvisation Therapy, where a 'given' 'serves to direct the group's attention to a limited area or facet of the modality or medium, while also stimulating them to explore all of the possibilities within those limits' (Bruscia 1987, p.175).

Decisions about appropriate and effective 'methods' of working in music therapy rely on integrating a number of elements from different theoretical frames, and will probably never be formulated into exact procedures. Taking into account the theoretical aspects of clinical pathology, philosophical orientation and existing music therapy methods, we can select from a range of musical techniques and thera-peutic methods (many of which are described in previous chapters) to decide an approach that will best serve the clients' needs. For example, if listening to music (receptive) is indicated as an appropriate tool, selecting, for example, 'Morning' from Edvard Grieg's *Peer Gynt Suite*, for a client with severe developmental disability, may have the function of relaxing and creating a lack of tension, whereas for a client with terminal illness, it may have the function of provoking imagery and reflection. To help with decisions in finding a relevant therapeutic approach, one needs to consider and evaluate the needs of clients on three different levels.

1.   *General needs (common to almost all clients)*

- To enter the security of a safe therapeutic environment.

- To enter a space where they can express themselves.

- To form a therapeutic relationship through music making with the therapist.

- To be offered a medium through which they can explore and develop their own process.

- To explore issues from their present and past life.

These are broad needs that can be generalized to almost every music therapy situation. Almost all therapists propose these as the needs of clients but sometimes limit their consideration of the purpose of the music therapy session to these broad aims. Therefore, it is useful to define needs related to discrete pathological problems, and needs related to the individual.

2.   *Needs telated to 'pathological' problems*

This involves defining the clients' needs from an understanding of their 'pathology' or personal characteristics that have caused them to be in therapy – such as learning difficulties, social impairment or personal crises, for example. Definition of these problems gives a clearer and more specific focus to the selection of methods, based on healthcare, educational or personal needs. For example, a client with autism typically displays ways of being and behaving that are related to the moderate or severe range of autism within the autistic continuum:

- difficulties in social interaction;
- difficulties in imagination and imaginative play;
- difficulties in communication;
- repetitive patterns of behaviour;
- difficulties in coping with change;
- abnormal and unusual motor and sensory disturbances.

This example gives some general descriptions of pathological difficulties within the framework of autism. One can generate a similar list of problems relating to other pathologies.

3.   *Individual needs*

From a therapeutic point of view, every client, irrespective of his or her diagnostic category, pathologic disorder, educational difficulty or personal and social problem is considered as an individual with a unique individual character and needs. Therefore the third level of defining needs relates to the individual's own life problems and needs:

- the client's own personality, history, personal identity, musical identity;
- the client's musical history;
- issues relating to the individual;
- personal characteristics in the relationship with the therapist;
- personal characteristics in the relationship with other clients in the group.

(Wigram 1996a, 1996b)

Using this model gives us a great deal to think about, and we often find in the therapy situation that it is challenging to take all these elements into consideration and at the same time act in an intuitive and free way with the clients. Sometimes the balance is wrong, and we become 'lost' in our clients and lack an overview or perspective of the general and specific needs. Music therapists don't typically begin a therapy session with a list of objectives to achieve based on these needs. I find it helpful to have a clear understanding and awareness of these different levels of needs, and they are 'present' during the therapy session. This allows me to act intuitively in therapy and while gaining further insight into the needs of the clients.

Table 8.2 Techniques and dynamics of improvisational music therapy

Improvisation		
Free and unstructured	**Themes**	**Structure of activity**
	Guided fantasy or story	Warm-up techniques
	Object	Instrumentally organized
	Picture or image	Musically organized
	Weather	
	Emotion	
The client's issues	The client's issues	
Medium	**Style of music**	**Degree of control**
Instruments	Atonal	Free
Percussion	Tonal	With initial playing rules or givens
+ piano	Modal	Partial structure
+ pitched percussion	Pentatonic	Full structure
Vocal dialogue	Stylistic	Partial/full direction
Vocal + instruments	Thematic extemporization	Gesture
Vocal alone	Extemporization	Music
Movement		Verbal
Movement + instrument		Conducted

No precise manual exists for the procedural application of music and music related media in therapy related to specific needs, because while there may be potentials to describe that application at a general level, individual differences prevent such a precise prescriptive approach. In the same way, improvisation applied in clinical practice can be understood as a spontaneously created 'recipe', where the therapist will utilize 'ingredients' from these different criteria to either respond to, or create a musical improvisation that would be relevant and therapeutically meaningful for the client.

The chart (Table 8.2) of techniques and dynamics of improvisational music therapy is more of a model from which choices can be made to introduce in therapy sessions, addressing the needs of the client. I first present the model, offering examples under the categories of Free and unstructured, Themes, Structure of activity, Medium, Style of music and Degree of control. There follow descriptions and explanations of the different methods. In choosing what might be used, a combination of different elements from different sections can be employed.

1.   *Free and unstructured*

This approach is used in therapy without any required or given play rules, musical structures or concrete material. The expression of feeling, emotion and state through musical improvisation occurs spontaneously without any specific or planned framework to the improvisation.

2.   *Themes*

Examples of themes that can be used to provide the frame or focus of the improvisation can include a guided fantasy, where the therapist, with or without the client's involvement, creates a fantasy in the music making, based on the idea of a 'tone-poem'. Another focus may be a story, where the client could tell a story verbally to start with, and then take this into an improvised experience. Other examples of where themes might come from are an object or painting, the weather on a particular day, or the weather as you would like it to be, an emotion, feeling or and abstract concept. Themes can vary from concrete to very abstract ideas. While these themes can be used as metaphors for the issue that one is working with, there is a direct approach by taking the client's point of reference and current issue as the focal theme of the improvisation. I have also said that comments and issues arising from warm-up experiences can be used as themes. The client's 'issue(s)' naturally and appropriately become the focus for an improvisation, although some care needs to be taken when placing a sensitive and potentially covered aspect of the client's life directly into focus. Defining the theme more as a metaphor might be less challenging.

3.   *Structure of activity*

Warm-ups

The warm-up ideas are well documented above, and the only one I have not specifically included or discussed here is empathic improvisation, which I have explained
in Chapter 4. These ideas can be applied when beginning sessions..

Instrumentally organized activity

This is where the play rules for a group improvisation provide structure according to
the instruments that may be used. Examples of this include focusing improvisation
purely on drums, where a range of different 'drum type' instruments are available
(congas, timpani, bongos, tambours, djembes, snare drums, etc.), or using pitched
percussion instruments such as xylophones, tone bars, glockenspiels or
metallophones. There could also be a wide range of instruments to differentiate
clients clearly from each other in the musical soundscape.

Musically organized activity

This is where the play rules for a group improvisation provide direction regarding
the nature and style of the music on which it is to be founded. For example, this can
involve giving a musical structure to an improvisation such as starting softly,
crescendoing to loud, then returning back to soft playing/vocalizing; establishing a
tonal or harmonic centre (pentatonic, modal, atonal) for the improvisation; or where
either the therapist or client(s) initiate a musical idea from which the improvisation
can develop.

4.   *Medium*

This will depend on the client's own choice, but also on some decision-making by
the therapist regarding what might be the most effective way of building a musical
relationship with the client. Working exclusively in a vocal dialogue or with voices
may be quite threatening for some clients, or entirely natural for others. If the client
chooses to play simple percussion instruments, then the therapist may choose to
support him or her on the same instruments, or may work from the piano. Receptive
techniques with recorded or live music include listening to some music that either
the client or the therapist has brought to the session, or the active technique of
moving or dancing to recorded music. Other therapeutic mediums such as
vibroacoustic therapy involve the client lying on a unit such as a bed or chair containing loudspeakers through which they can feel the physical sensation of sound, in
conjunction with low frequency sound. Contrastingly, Guided Imagery and Music

involves the client imaging while in a state of receptive awareness to specific pro-
grammed selections of predominately classical music.

5.   *Style of music*

The music used may be atonal, tonal, dissonant or modal, but could also have additional stylistic frameworks such as melodic improvisation, pentatonic improvisation,
or Spanish and Middle Eastern styles of improvisation.

6.   *Degree of control*

The control or direction over what is happening musically in the session may be
determined by the client or the therapist. The range shown in this section of Table
8.2 varies from free improvisation without any form of control to conducted improvisation, which involves almost complete control. Initial structure may be determined by playing rules that can be defined by the client or the therapist together,
where they may decide there are some elements that they are going to include in the
improvisation.

Partial structure leading to full structure is a technique where the therapist and
the client decide how they are going to begin playing, what might happen in the
middle of their improvisation, and how they are going to end, and could also include
defined musical elements, such as beginning with a steady pulse, accelerating to an
uneven tempo and chaotic rhythmic structures.

Partial to full direction gives the control element either to the client or the
therapist who can, during improvisation, direct their partner in a specific way. For
example, I might give the client the opportunity to decide when he would like me to
play at any time during the improvisation, and indicate this by touching me or
looking at me, or by stopping playing himself.

A conducted degree of control involves the client or the therapist actively 'conducting' an individual with some basic symbols or signs indicating how he or she
wants them to play – for example, raising their arms above their head when they
want the volume to increase, crouching down and making small movements with
their hands if they want a soft, gentle sound. This method was also described as a
warm-up (see above).

Combinations of elements could result in the following frameworks:

- free and unstructured improvisation through a vocal dialogue using an
  internal medium

- an improvisation of a picture using pitched percussion instruments in a
  pentatonic mode, thus incorporating partial structure

- using an emotional theme, listening to recorded, tonal pre-composed
  music with a feedback period afterwards.

The ideas I have listed in Table 8.2, and the explanations of some of this material form only a part of the wide variety of techniques and ideas one can introduce into music therapy sessions. These techniques can be at a conceptual level, or they can be specifically musical or interactively structured. The choice depends entirely on the client's needs, the phase of work that has been reached in the therapy process, and the therapist's intuition or the process or musical relationship that is being developed.

8.3 Concrete, abstract and emotional themes

This thematic model is based on the idea that the client produces material that is used in improvisational experiences with the therapist and acts as the focal point for therapeutic engagement and work. The material described in Chapter 7 is predominantly musical material. However, the play rules that include developing themes for the clients to use as a focus for improvisation can also include concepts, objects, images, feelings and ideas that can be applied as concrete or abstract themes. This section gives examples of this for use in both individual and group improvisation. As the influence of the therapist has been addressed in earlier chapters concerned with defining and applying therapeutic methods, the effect of the therapeutic relationship for the therapist will briefly be discussed, with reference to a clinical situation and a clinical example.

One model of clinical work with verbal clients involves a discussion of the issues with which the clients are working, the problems they have in their everyday life or the difficulties they are encountering as a result of their pathology becoming the focus of the therapeutic work. This can become the focus of the improvisation, and so the 'theme' for the improvisation can be something relating to a concrete idea, an abstract concept or even an emotion or feeling with which the client is working.

Given my experience over many years in the field of learning disability, I have found themes for improvisation tend to be more concrete, and a different music therapy approach is appropriate. The more abstract the idea, the more the client has to be able to understand the symbolization of that idea or its metaphoric significance within music making. This is not easy with clients who have learning disability. However, even some quite concrete concepts, such as the weather or relationships with people, could be used in a fairly straightforward way as themes for improvisation.

Concrete themes can include objects that are easy to observe and see and that have relevance and meaning to the client. Therefore ideas that can be taken from pictures, sculptures or everyday objects such as telephones, televisions, lights can form the focus for the improvisation. Environmental images can be the focus for the development of an improvisation, such as:

- the woods at night;
- staying on a beach;
- a sea journey;
- lakes and mountains;
- a busy city;
- a party.

There are many possibilities and these ideas can act as metaphors for issues with which the client is working.

Some of the more interactive yet concrete improvisational themes that can be used in working in this approach in music therapy with individuals and with groups are:

- having a conversation;
- having an argument;
- starting in a safe place – going to a dangerous place – going back to a safe place;
- sunrise – the dawn;
- sunset – twilight;
- going on a journey – making contact with others.

Using these themes, and the many others that can emerge from client/therapist work, one can build improvisations using the musical and therapeutic parameters described above. It is appropriate to use some of the musical parameters to help with structure where one is working with more abstract themes. Conversely, where one is working on a purely spontaneous and intuitive level, no structure is necessary and the theme itself should be the only 'playing rule' in order to allow totally spontaneous and novel music to emerge as a consequence.

Improvisations on emotions and feelings

Very typically in music therapy one is exploring emotional issues with clients. They may be dealing with emotional blocks, over-emotional behaviour, a lack of emotional behaviour or emotional issues relating to unfinished business from the past. Consequently, it is sometimes useful to use emotions or moods for themes of improvisation.

In the entrance tests at Aalborg University Masters programme in music therapy, we often ask the students to make an improvisation using some form of emotional mood material. We suggest that they find a way of moving from one mood or emotion to another – creating a sort of 'binary' style of improvisation (A to B).

Some themes that could be used for improvisations based on emotions or moods are:

- feeling afraid going to feeling confident;
- sadness going to peace;
- frustration going to determination.

Themes can be employed that contain and relate to emotions and moods in improvisational experiences with clients. I have found this particularly important when working with people with autism, autistic spectrum disorder and Asperger's syndrome where the recognition of emotions and moods in others is severely impaired due to social impairments and difficulties in reading and understanding facial expression and tone of voice. Consequently, I have explored in my clinical work how to help clients recognize mood qualities in music and used some levels of extremes in the musical parameters, such as very soft, slow and limited movement in the music to illustrate sadness, together with fast, loud and excited movements in the music to illustrate happiness or excitement.

8.4 Thematic improvisation, musical form, transference and counter-transference

The final section of this chapter delves briefly into the complex area of musical form, and how that relates to the structure of spontaneous improvisation and the therapeutic process. The therapeutic relationship is discussed in the context of the development through musical experiences, and a short review is made of the ways music therapists have considered transference and counter-transference in the music therapy process. Taking the influence of musical form first, the possible structures that emerge, or are deliberately created, in improvisation, can reflect and symbolize aspects of the therapeutic relationship.

One such structure could be as follows:

Table 8.3 Sonata form as a metaphor in therapy

Process	(slow) Introduction	Exposition	Development	Recapitulation	Coda
A single improvisation	Exploring the instrument or voice Transition to….	Creating some musical ideas and then responding with other musical ideas to each other Transition to…	Trying out new musical directions, using ideas from the exposition, but extending Transition to…	Going back to the ideas in the exposition, especially the ones that were liked, and that 'worked' Transition to…	Finding a way to end the music: slowing down; cadencing; agreeing a musical end
Making a friend	Meeting – Cautious at first; asking each other questions; 'sizing' each other up; first impressions Transition to…	Finding shared interests; sharing ideas; sharing experiences; share understanding; Transition to…	Exploring some new directions; perhaps finding areas where you differ; learning new things about the other; being apart? Transition to…	Re-establishing shared ideas; resolving differences; returning to familiar and agreed likes and preferences; re-uniting Transition to…	There may be no 'Coda' in an ongoing friendship.
The therapeutic relationship	Meeting; becoming acquainted; establishing basis of therapeutic relationship Transition to…	Learning about each other's identity; testing each other; establishing roles, functions and boundaries Transition to…	Meeting challenges; discovering new dimensions; experiencing conflicts; new roles? Transition to…	Consolidating and confirming; reflecting on the value of the relationship; experiencing and understanding the developed 'history'; coming to an end Transition to…	Ending the relationship; thinking about the future; finishing the process; saying goodbye
Process of therapy	Referral; observing, exploring, perceiving and considering; identifying areas of therapeutic need. Transition to…	Beginning to work on issues; making a direction for the therapy; first phase of therapy Transition to…	Working in new directions; trying out new ideas; therapeutic challenges; second phase of therapy Transition to…	Re-establishing the aims or direction of therapy; returning to earlier issues and themes; consolidating the progress and process Transition to…	Coming to the end of therapy; issues of closure; saying goodbye

1. Searching for a theme.

2. Initiation of a theme.

3. Response to a theme.

4. Development of a theme.

5. Changing or extending a theme.

6. Recapitulation of a theme.

7. Closing a theme.

From the point of view of musical analysis, this can be seen as closely resembling sonata or symphonic form. I am not suggesting that improvisations will normally develop in sonata form, as they could equally be structured in binary, ternary or rondo form, or theme and variations. However, I have found it helpful to look at a number of aspects of the therapeutic process in terms of musical form. The development of musical style, and our everyday understanding and use of music is significantly affected by all the different formal structures in its composition. The creation of music through improvisation is inevitably influenced by our cultural musical background, our likes and dislikes and our musical competency. One can also add that the professional competency of music therapists is half founded in their musical training, and applying the knowledge and skill we have developed as musicians will strengthen the musical identity and professional identity of the music therapist.

A single improvisation, a session, a series of sessions, and the development of the therapeutic relationship in either a single session or a number of sessions can be looked at and analysed in the context of musical form. At a more simple level, the AB or ABA of binary and ternary form provides a safe framework in music and in the relationship. Rondo form (ABACADAEA) provides an opportunity creatively to move away from a theme and then return to it. The 'theme' becomes a grounding element, both in the music and in the relationship. This is equally true in theme and variations, with the difference that the theme becomes the focus for creative improvisation and exploration. Tone poems and symphonic poems, common in the nineteenth and early twentieth century, provide another model, where the music (or the relationship) is developed through a story or picture.

To go back to the earlier reference to sonata or symphonic form, this can be understood as a metaphor for the development, within an improvisation, of the musical relationship between client and therapist, the therapeutic process in one session or over a whole series of sessions, or even the way we make friends. Table 8.3

demonstrates this using different examples including improvisation, friendship, therapeutic relationship and therapy process.

Both therapists and clients make use of form and structure either for security, or unconsciously to mark their own boundaries. Therefore within these musical boundaries, and in the context of the therapeutic relationship through music, the processes of transference and counter-transference frequently occur during any one of these stages (Wigram 1995a).

Transference

For an understanding of transference, I will draw on the work of Juliette Alvin (Alvin 1975; Bruscia 1987, pp.73–108) and Mary Priestley (1975, 1994) as pioneers who all incorporated psychoanalytic thinking in their work, and influenced generations of music therapists. Alvin proposes the concept that the music and the instruments are the main objects of transference rather than the therapist. Therefore, instead of projecting their feelings onto the therapist, clients will use the instruments and sounds to work through any negative feelings they have towards significant other people in their lives. This concept enables the therapist to allow the musical instrument to become the object of the client's transference, and all their love or anger; positive and negative transference respectively can be put into a musical 'box'. This leaves us with the question of to whom that music is being directed. When a therapist responds to a client's music, he or she is entering into a relationship with the client's music, and therefore with the client. However, it does enable the therapist to facilitate a three-way connection: therapist; music; client. Alvin proposes that this theory protects the client – therapist relationship from any negative transference, and the therapist does not need to work through all the client's conflicts with others, and can allow the client to build up the kind of relationship he needs to have in his life (Bruscia 1987).

Bruscia describes Mary Priestley's understanding of transference as a process where a client uses the therapist as an object to work through important unfinished business from a previous relationship. The features of transference include repetition of the past, and distortion of the present. Warm, loving feelings to a therapist can be a catalyst of therapeutic change, while hostility with underlying anger and hate can stimulate resistance and aggression, but also a working through of resentments coming from previous or present relationships (Bruscia 1987).

In thematic improvisation, I have observed and experienced this positive and negative transference, and it can be described in appropriate musical events. The initiation of a theme by a client or student can be a challenge to me, a way of saying 'try and respond to that'. The harmony might be rigid and inflexible, or the rhythm broken and patchy. Either musical element may be a form of transference. In the developmental section of thematic improvisation, the way a client or student tries to come close to me musically, and blend into our 'thematic adventure' can be felt as a strong, positive transference.

Counter-transference

In discussing counter-transference, I will refer specifically to the work of Mary Priestley and Kenneth Bruscia. Priestley describes counter-transference as a process where the therapist comes to the therapy situation with feelings, attitudes, motivations, values, beliefs and behaviour patterns. She identifies two types of reaction: first, the therapist's unconscious reaction to the client and the client's transference; second, the therapist's identification with the client. In the second effect, the therapist identifies with unconscious feelings or internal objects of the client that give him/her insight into the client's hidden inner life (Bruscia 1987).

In musical improvisation, Priestley uses the technique of empathic counter-transference, which she describes as one of the most important tools of the analytical music therapist. Improvisation requires the therapist to stay attuned to his own feelings, particularly as they relate to those being expressed by the client. (Priestley 1975).

Bruscia defines various forms of counter-transference:

Positive: when the therapist can observe his/her personal reactions in therapy and use them to benefit the client.

Negative: when the therapist is unaware of his/her reactions to the client, or is unwilling to observe them.

He also talks about empathic counter-transference, where the therapist identifies with the client and experiences what the client is experiencing to some degree. Therefore, in this instance, they are both subjects in a relationship, focusing on the same object. Bruscia gives further examples of somatic, emotional, behavioural and musical counter-transference. Musical counter-transference in particular can be understood as a process where 'the therapist's reactions to the client are manifested in the way he selects or makes music within the therapy situation' (Bruscia 1994).

These concepts are only briefly explored, although the influence of unconscious feelings and emotions is profound and significant in the applied use of clinical improvisation. Learning musical techniques and therapeutic methods is the first stage in a long process that leads on to emerging clinical competency and, ultimately, clinical expertise. Therapists become fluent and confident in their flexible and dexterous use of method in therapy, and the musical techniques described in earlier chapters become second nature. However, each new client is an individual, with individual needs. Experience and competency does not defend a therapist from feelings of resistance, negativity, bias, over-supportiveness and even inadequacy. These relate to personal characteristics, past history and current events in the life of the therapist, and will affect the nature of improvisation in the therapeutic process. The consequences are to some extent inevitable, and the most appropriate and 'professional' way to manage such powerful and influential experiences is to maintain awareness, understanding and insight into their emergence, presence and value.

CHAPTER 9

Two Different Methods for Analyzing and Reporting Improvised Music

Introduction

This last chapter is concerned with how we can analyse musical material, whether from pre-composed music or a piece of improvisation. The methods and techniques I have described in the last eight chapters give some clear frameworks, and make it easier to identify existing structure, style, dynamic and meaning in the musical material. However, improvised music is frequently the result of spontaneous, unplanned music making, and therefore the product is, by nature, unpredictable. I think that one can approach the analysis of improvised music, and indeed all other forms of music by asking two essential questions:

- How can I describe this music?

- What is the function of this music?

This may sound reductionist, yet these two questions actually encapsulate many other questions that need to be addressed. Making a good enough description of the musical material (question 1) means considering all the parameters and elements of music, as well as the style of performance, and the moods and associations the music might provoke. Exploring the function of the music leads into a far more complex process applied in music therapy in order to analyse the musical material in relation to a number of therapeutic parameters or expectations. Here the structure, style, engagement and interaction that goes on in shared music making between therapists and clients, or by a client on his/her own, are the focus of the analysis, drawing out implications and conclusions about issues relating to therapy process.

The first question can be answered by using an adequate and inclusive model of musical analysis in order to make a comprehensive and adequate description. The purpose of this is to do no more nor less than to give an overall verbal description of a piece of music that is specific enough for someone to be able to understand what that music sounds like.

9.1 Analysis of music for a musical purpose

A good model for music analysis has been developed by Dr Denise Erdonmez Grocke during her doctoral research into Guided Imagery and Music (GIM). I was involved in the later stages of this research, during which she developed a model of musical analysis in order to seek information about the structure of the music in a music programme immediately prior to a 'pivotal moment' in the therapeutic process. Erdonmez Grocke was particularly interested to explore common aspects that could be seen in music that underpinned these pivotal moments described by subjects in her research, and so needed a comprehensive music analysis tool to find similarities and dissimilarities in four pieces of music (Erdonmez Grocke 1999). Drawing on the list of relevant musical elements formulated but not published by Bonny (the founder of GIM) Erdonmez Grocke then developed a much expanded and more comprehensive music analysis tool, consisting of twelve categories of musical elements, and a further three categories concerned with mood, symbolic and associational meaning and performance. In total, there was a list of 63 sub-components under these 15 headings.

Verification indicated that the tool Erdonmez Grocke developed was inclusive and detailed enough to satisfy content validity, as well as being criterion-related and with construct validity. In addition, part of the process of this research involved validating this tool, by determining which of the 15 categories and 63 components were difficult to assess, or were too general to be precise. For example, elements such as whether the structure of the music was predominantly simple or complex, whether intervals were conventional or unconventional, the pitch range of the instruments and the level of resonance in the timbre were difficult to evaluate, and were excluded from the final analysis tool. Moreover, in the process of analysing and verifying using this tool, we found additional elements that needed to be included. Table 9.1 is the revised Structural Model for Musical Analysis that was developed out of this research.

Table 9.1 A Structural Model for Music Analysis (SMMA) (Erdonmez Grocke 1999)

1. Style and Form

   1.1. Period of composition: e.g. baroque, classical, romantic; impressionist; 20th century (from 1910–)

   1.2 Form: e.g. sonata form; ABA; theme and variations; rhapsodic form; fugue; tone poem

   1.3 Structure: predominantly simple or complex

2. Texture

   2.1 Consistently thick/thin or variable

   2.2. Monophonic; homophonic; polyphonic

3. Time

   3.1 Meter: 2/4 or 4/4; 3/4 or 5/4, etc.

   3.2 Complexity and variability in meter.

   3.3 Silences; rests; pauses

4. Rhythmic features

   4.1 Underlying pulse of the work – consistent/inconsistent

   4.2 Important rhythmic motifs

   4.3 Repetition in rhythmic motifs

   4.4. Variability in rhythm – predictable/unpredictable

   4.5 Syncopation

5. Tempo

   5.1 Fast; slow; moderato; allegro, etc.

   5.2 Alterations in tempi: change of meter; use of accelerandi and ritardandi

6. Tonal features

   6.1 Key in which the work is written

   6.2 Key structure; diatonic; modal.

   6.3 Major/minor alternations

   6.4 Chromaticism

   6.5 Modulation points

7. Melody

7.1 The main themes in the selection (1st theme, 2nd theme with development or variations)

7.2 Significant melodic fragments

7.3 The structure of the melody: propinquity; step-wise progressions; large intervalic leaps

7.4 Significant intervals (e.g., fall of an octave in a melody). *Intervals: conventional or unconventional*

7.5 Shape – rounded, ascending, descending

7.6 Length of phrases: symmetrical, short, long

7.7 *Pitch range of instruments*

8. Embellishments, ornamentation and articulation

8.1 Embellishments to the melodic line

8.2 Trills; appoggiaturas

8.3 Accentuation: marcato; accents; detached bowing

8.4 Pizzicato/legato

8.6 Use of mute

9. Harmony

9.1 Predominantly consonant, or dissonant

9.2 Consonance/dissonance alternation within the selection

9.3 Significant harmonic progressions

9.4 Rich harmonies

9.5 Predictable harmonies (e.g. I; IV; V progression)

9.6 Unpredictable harmonies

9.7 Cadence points – perfect; imperfect; interrupted

10. Timbre and quality of instrumentation

10.1 Solo instrument: instrumental; vocal

10.2 Accompaniment to solo instrument/voice: orchestral; choral; other instrument

10.3 Small group – e.g. quartet, combinations of instruments

10.4 Instrument groups used in orchestration (strings, woodwinds, brass, percussion, harp) creating timbral colour

10.5 Interplay between instruments and instrument groups

10.6 Layering effects (adding and reducing instrument parts)

11. Volume

11.1 Predominantly loud or soft – alternations between/gradation between

11.2 Special effects of volume: pianissimo; fortissimo; Sforzandi

12. Intensity

12.1 Tension/release

12.2 Crescendi, building to peak, and resolution

12.3 Tension in harmony, texture, etc., and resolution

12.4 Delayed resolution or absent resolution

12.5 Ambiguity resolved or unresolved

13. Mood

13.1 Predominant mood, as depicted by melody, harmony and predominant instrument

13.2 Feelings and emotions represented.

14. Symbolic/associational

14.1 Culturally specific associations – e.g. Vaughan-Williams' English idioms

14.2 Metaphoric associations

15. Performance

15.1 Quality of performance (including technique of the performers)

15.2 Stylistic interpretation – artistic merit

15.3 Articulation of feeling and emotion

It is worth remembering that this tool was developed to analyse the music used in GIM – which is predominantly classical and orchestral. Consequently, the music is often very complex, for example in some of the late romantic works used in the GIM programmes. Therefore making analysis of the 'pitch range of instruments' would be rather futile. However, in more simple forms of improvisational music, the elements that were excluded from the SMMA for the doctoral study because of the complexity of the music could easily be relevant for analysing improvised music. For example, examining an improvisation and determining whether it has a predominantly simple structure, conventional or unconventional intervals, and the pitch range of the instruments used might be very relevant information. So I have re-included these aspects (*in italics*) in the above table for optional use. Nevertheless, as it stands it contains enough elements in the form of a 'checklist' to undertake an analysis of a piece of improvisation that is primarily concerned with describing the music.

The last three sections (13,14 and 15) are likely to elicit quite subjective impressions. Performance as a category may also seem inappropriate for a structural analysis of improvised music. However there is an element of 'performance' in the way some clients make music, so it may be relevant to offer a comment on that. Erdonmez Grocke herself says that the integrity, authenticity and excellence of performance is, in any event, a subjective measurement, and relates to how convincing the performance was to the listener. These items were excluded from the final revised version. Aspects concerned with quality, stylistic interpretation and the articulation of feelings and emotions in the way the client 'performs' music were retained – which could have their own relevance for commenting on improvised music.

The important thing to realize about this analysis tool is that it is a set of criteria, some or all of which can be used to describe adequately a part or whole of an improvisation. It is not a standardized precision tool that comes with a procedure or set of instructions attached that must be followed, and Erdonmez Grocke has not given guidelines she expects users to follow. Rather it functions as a frame by which to determine the presence and quality of musical and some non-musical parameters in order to give a comprehensive and adequate description and to answer the first question in analysing music.

To end this section, I will provide an example of how this tool works in practice drawn from Erdonmez Grocke's doctoral thesis on a piece of pre-composed music, in this case the slow second movement of Beethoven's Violin Concerto where, following the SMMA by Erdonmez Grocke, and the verification by myself, Erdonmez Grocke gives a final, condensed, phenomenological description:

> The music is written for solo violin with orchestra, and is in a major key. Its structure is simple, comprising two themes with variations. There is a dialogue between the violin and the orchestra, and between the violin, and clarinet, bassoon and horn. The solo violin part often transcends the orchestra, with embellishments in the high register. The mood is quiet and peaceful, but also expansive. The harmonic structure of the work is consonant, and the melodic line and harmonic sequences are predictable. There are no unexpected progressions, and the accompaniment is supportive throughout. The strings provide a section of pizzicato in the accompaniment which contrasts with the legato line of the solo violin. The violin solo drifts away at the end. (Erdonmez Grocke 1999, p.213)

For a further example of the importance of musical analysis for a muscial purpose, from earlier research I have conducted into the relaxing and therapeutic effects of low frequency sound and sedative music (Wigram 1996c; Wigram and Dileo 1997), I would like to add one further dimension and tool. In order to select and describe music that can be generally described as relaxing or stimulating, I have formulated criteria for the elements one typically finds in stimulatory and sedative music, and have based the conceptual framework for this on the potential predictability and stability of the music. The table that follows (Table 9.2) is an attempt to define the characteristics of music, and how it can be played. This can also act as a guide for improvising with the intention of promoting stimulation or relaxation.

Table 9.2 Potentials in Stimulatory and Sedative Music (PSSM) (adapted from Wigram 2002b)

Potential elements in stimulating music

- Unpredictable changes in tempo
- Unpredictable or sudden changes in: volume, rhythm, timbre, pitch and harmony
- Wide variations in texture in the music
- Unnexpected dissonance
- Unexpected accents
- Harsh timbres
- Lack of structure and form in the music
- Sudden accelerandos, ritardandos, crescendos and diminuendos
- Unexpected breaks in the music

Potential elements in sedative music

- Stable tempo
- Stability or only gradual changes in: volume, rhythm, timbre, pitch and harmony
- Consistent texture
- Predictable harmonic modulation
- Appropriate cadences
- Predictable melodic lines
- Repetition of material
- Structure and form

- Gentle timbres

- Few accents

Compared to Erdonmez Grocke's more comprehensive SMMA this is a more specific choice of certain parameters to answer a narrower question. The question here is not how can one describe the music, but is the music stimulatory or sedative in style?

The SMMA and the PSSM are tools for analysing music, but they also provide a frame for the creation of music. In developing musical skills to use in clinical improvisation, music therapy students and qualified practitioners learn how the balanced and effective use of these elements can be made in a very sensitive and subtle way to engage and help patients. Some clients *need* the stability and safety of predictable music, for example, people with psychotic disturbance, whose world is chaotic and disconnected. Others, for example patients with autism, learning disability, or anxiety neuroses, *need* to develop abilities to cope with an unpredictable world, and this can begin in developing adaptability to unpredictable musical experiences. So the elements of music that can determine the effect in receptive music therapy also play an important role in active music making with clients.

9.2 Analysis of music for a therapeutic purpose

Returning now to the second of the two questions I posed above, when presenting the results of a music therapy assessment, or a period of music therapy, the documentation of musical material, and the analysis of the musical experience that has been present during the session(s) with clients has specific connections to therapeutic issues. Therefore the analysis involves examining the 'function' of the music in order to establish connections to pathological problems and therapeutic process. From the literature, and in examining current clinical practice, we can see that very few 'general' models, let alone 'standardized' models, of assessment have been developed. In music therapy, scales (tools) for assessment and evaluation developed to date have focused on a variety of aspects of the music therapy process, including purely musical analysis as described above (Erdonmez Grocke 1999; Wigram 2002b); musical interaction and dynamics (Pavlicevic 1995; Skewes 2001); response, relationship and musical communicativeness (Nordoff and Robbins 1977); diagnosis (Raijmaekers 1993; Wigram 2002a); psychological function (Sikström and Skille 1995); cognitive, perceptual, motor and visual skills (Grant 1995); sound-musical profiles (Di Franco 1999); and the analysis of improvised music (Bruscia 1987) to name but a few.

While these scales or criteria for assessment typically rely on subjective opinion and, to my knowledge trials involving observer reliability or verification have not taken place, they are often detailed, well thought out and with appropriate clinical applicability for a specific population. However, apart from the Nordoff-Robbins Scales, there is no systematic and widespread use of any one of these models, which is a shame considering the extent and detail of some of the parameters that can be used. Typically, therapists will collect one or more of the types of data in Table 9.3 in order to make their evaluation in any one of these models of assessment. The term behaviour is used here as a descriptor of all types of behaviour: physiological, emotional, cognitive, unconscious, etc., and includes an understanding of human behaviour from psychotherapeutic, medical and behavioural traditions.

Table 9.3 Data gathering in assessment and evaluation

Musical data	(examples of musical events/musical characteristics)
Musical behavioural data	(examples of client's behaviour without musical description)
Behavioural data	(characteristics of general behaviour in music therapy)
Interpretative data	(interpretation of client's musical and general behaviour supported or not supported by musical or behavioural data)
Comparative data	(comparison of client's behaviour in music therapy with behaviour in other situations)

One assessment procedure that focuses specifically on musical elements as the basis for analysing change or lack of change in clients is the Improvisation Assessment Profiles (IAPs), (Bruscia 1987), and this is the tool I think is the most comprehensive and relevant way to explain the function of the music. Despite the fact that IAPs have been in the literature for some years there is quite a limited use of this assessment method currently, perhaps because it is a complex, detailed and extensive method of analysis.

In the complete set of IAPs, Bruscia has defined six specific areas of potential analysis: autonomy, variability, integration, salience, tension and congruence. Each profile provides criteria for analysing improvisation, and the criteria for all the profiles form a 'continuum of five gradients or levels, ranging from one extreme or polarity to its opposite' (Bruscia 1987, p.406).

To use these profiles in an economic and effective way to analyse musical material, it is necessary to follow the recommendations and guidelines that Bruscia offers for using IAPs. Part of this process involves reducing the amount of material to

Table 9.4 IAP autonomy profile

1 = Dependent
2 = Follower
3 = Partner
4 = Leader
5 = Resister

- Rhythmic ground
- Rhythmic figure

- Tonal and melodic
- Harmonic

- Texture

- Phrasing

- Volume
- Timbre

- Programme/lyrics

Table 9.5 IAP variability profile

1 = Rigid
2 = Stable
3 = Variable
4 = Contrasting
5 = Random

- Tempo
- Meter/subdivisions
- Rhythmic figure

- Melodic figure
- Tonal ground
- Harmonic
- Style

- Texture: Overall
- Texture: Roles
- Texture: Register
- Texture: Configurations

- Phrasing
- Volume
- Timbre

- Body

- Lyrics

be analysed to that which is both pertinent and essential, and then choosing the appropriate profile(s) to apply. The practical application of IAPs has been developed for both quantitative and qualitative analysis. I want to explain the method by which I apply this comprehensive assessment tool, describing both the decisions I take, and the use of the parameters Bruscia has incorporated for analysis.

Of Bruscia's six areas for analysis, the two profiles that I use most frequently for the analysis of musical material with children who have communication disorder are autonomy and variability (Wigram 1999b,c, 2000a, 2001), and so I will use these two for the purposes of explaining the method I use in this analysis. For the original and comprehensive text on the Improvisation Assessment Profiles, see Bruscia 1987. The profiles and scales for autonomy and variability are described in Tables 9.4 and 9.5.

> 'The autonomy profile deals with the kinds of role relationships formed between the improvisers. The scales within the profile describe the extent to which each musical element and component is used to lead or follow the other' (Bruscia 1987, p.405).

> 'The variability profile deals with how sequential aspects of the music are organised and related. Scales within the profile describe the extent to which each musical element or component stays the same or changes' (Bruscia 1987, p.404).

In relation to clinical work, I have found these two profiles are useful in differentiating between children who have autism or some other variant of pervasive development disorder or communication disorder. Autonomy helps one look closely at the inter-personal events that are going on, particularly the readiness of a child to work together with me, take turns, share and act as a partner, or the child's propensity for resisting suggestions or becoming extremely dependent and reliant. Variability can illustrate at an inter- and intra-musical level the child's capacity for creativity, or evidence of a child's rigid or repetitive way of playing that might support a diagnosis on the autistic continuum.

Practical application

To use these profiles in an economic and effective way to analyse musical material, one needs first to study the recommendations and guidelines that Bruscia offers for using the IAPs. Essentially one has to follow a process of reducing the amount of material to be analysed to that which is both pertinent and essential, and then choosing the appropriate method within the IAPs to do it.

1. Consider whether one is focusing on intra-musical or inter-musical events, or both.

2. Choose the relevant profiles for analysis, related to either the focus of the therapy, or the questions raised for the assessment.

3. Review the entire session to be analysed, and select sections or improvisations from the session that contain some of the most relevant material that will reap pertinent and valuable information when analysed. (Bruscia 1987, pp.418–421)

I have added to this some criteria that helped me particularly in the process of diagnostic assessment, and also to continue to reduce the amount of analysis that is necessary to produce some relevant information through which one can interpret and evaluate what is happening musically.

1. Based on issues related to the referral or the child's behaviour, and having reviewed musical events and the musical behaviour of the child in this session, I choose the particular musical elements on the scale it is most relevant to use in the analysis. The scales are quite detailed and lengthy, and it may be beneficial to select out, for example, rhythm, volume and phrasing as three particular elements that will be fruitful for analysis.

2. I use an event-charting system, where, on looking at a video recording or listening to an audiotape, I search for musical events that can be categorized using the gradients of the profiles. I have generated a form for undertaking this analysis (Table 9.6).

Typically I will select two or three sections of the session for analysis, and then select the elements of the scale that I wish to focus on and write them in under each gradient of the two different profiles. Watching the sections I have chosen to analyse on video, often two to three times, I will score the number of events in the boxes where I can see, for example, variability in tempo. Bruscia provides a very rich resource in his descriptors of types of musical material that come under these gradients where he describes the five different levels of either variability or autonomy (Bruscia 1987, pp.430–431, 445–447).

Using the improvisation assessment profiles for event-based analysis

Purpose: To identify events in musical improvisation using specific profiles and items from the musical scales.

   Procedure for analysis:

Stage 1. Select a short section of improvisation for analysis.

Stage 2. Decide which profile(s) to use based on the focus of therapy/nature of client – therapist relationship or client's music.

Stage 3. Watch or listen to the extract from the improvisation again and decide which musical/other parameters will be monitored from the profile (maximum three).

Stage 4. Choose one parameter to begin with and watch the video again.

Stage 5. *Events:* Make a tick in the box *each time* an event occurs in the improvisation. Pause the tape while doing so, i.e. if the client changes tempo, and the therapist follows, and the client stays stable for a few seconds in the new tempo, make a tick under:
Autonomy:'Leader':Rhythmic ground *or* Variability: 'Variable or contrasting': Tempo

Stage 6. Where relevant (and interesting) notate any clear 'leitmotifs/themes' at the bottom for future reference in reports.

Stage 7. When you have finished this parameter, choose the second parameter and analyse the events again (stages 4–6).

Stage 8. Add up the events in each box, and put total scores onto the form.

Stage 9. Interpret the scores for this section of improvisation in relation to the aims of therapy, etc.

Stage 10. If another profile is to be applied, repeat process from stages 3–9.

Table 9.6 Event Based Analysis (EBA) raw score sheet

Name.................................... Date.......................

Profile:...............................

	Gradient 1	Gradient 2	Gradient 3	Gradient 4	Gradient 5
Musical parameter					

Table 9.6 is the raw score sheet within which I place the gradients of the chosen profile, and the chosen musical parameters from Bruscia's scales. I record with a mark or a tick each time an event occurs. Depending on both the musical and the therapeutic situation, events can be identified by frequency alone, or by frequency and duration. In many cases, the complexity and multi-layered nature of the music in improvisations makes it quite difficult to identify the duration of an event. For example, you may note when a client (or therapist) has changed tempo, and whether the other follows – but how long that new tempo remains stable (duration of the event) can be difficult to see when other related or unrelated events are occurring simultaneously. Therefore, for some purposes it is enough to record a moment when an event starts. Following collection of the scores, the totals can then be transferred to another form where an overview of what is occurring can be seen. Table 9.7 gives an example from a client whose case has been previously reported in the *Nordisk Tidsskrift for Musikterapi 8* (Wigram 1999b) where the total scores can be seen.

Table 9.7 Summary IAP for a 5-year-old boy with language delay (Bruscia 1987, adapted by Wigram, 1996)

Patient's name: Barry   Date: _____

Analysis:
Section 1: Piano+drums
Section 2: Piano+metallophone
Section 3: Piano duet

Autonomy				Variability			
Dependant	1	2	3	**Rigid**	1	2	3
Rhythmic ground	2	-	-	Tempo	-	-	-
Melody	3	-	-	Melody	-	-	-
Timbre	-	-	-	Timbre	-	-	-
Follower				**Stable**			
Rhythmic ground	12	3	2	Tempo	7	3	1
Melody	6	-	-	Melody	5	2	-
Timbre	2	-	1	Timbre	2	7	-
Partner				**Variable**			
Rhythmic ground	3	2	2	Tempo	8	5	3
Melody	1	1	3	Melody	6	3	2
Timbre	1	-	-	Timbre	8	1	5
Leader				**Contrasting**			
Rhythmic ground	4	7	3	Tempo	3	2	2
Melody	1	4	-	Melody	1	1	3
Timbre	1	-	-	Timbre	8	1	5
Resister				**Random**			
Rhythmic ground	-	-	4	Tempo	-	-	1
Melody	-	-	-	Melody	-	-	-
Timbre	-	-	2	Timbre	-	-	-

Table 9.8 Summary IAP for an 11-year-old boy with classical autism

Patient's name: Daniel　　　　　　Date: _____

Analysis:
Section 1: Opening+Drum
Section 2: Guitar, Piano, Cymbal
Section 3: Vocal/Mic.

Autonomy				Variability			
Dependant	**1**	**2**	**3**	**Rigid**	**1**	**2**	**3**
Rhythmic ground	-	-	-	Tempo	12	7	-
Rhythmic figure	-	-	-	Rhythmic figure	8	3	-
Timbre	-	-	-	Timbre	3	-	-
Follower				**Stable**			
Rhythmic ground	3	-	-	Tempo	-	-	2
Rhythmic figure	-	-	-	Rhythmic figure	-	-	3
Timbre	-	-	-	Timbre	-	-	2
Partner				**Variable**			
Rhythmic ground	2	3	5	Tempo	2	-	-
Rhythmic figure	1	-	-	Rhythmic figure	1	-	-
Timbre	-	-	-	Timbre	-	3	-
Leader				**Contrasting**			
Rhythmic ground	2	1	1	Tempo	-	-	-
Rhythmic figure	1	-	-	Rhythmic figure	-	-	-
Timbre	-	-	-	Timbre	-	-	-
Resister				**Random**			
Rhythmic ground	9	4	1	Tempo	-	-	-
Rhythmic figure	7	3	1	Rhythmic figure	-	-	-
Timbre	10	7	2	Timbre	2	-	-

The data in Table 9.7 provided evidence of musical interaction, some emerging musical independence in the scores in musical leadership and a lack of rigidity. Therefore this analysis supported a diagnosis of significant language delay rather than autism. The events in Table 9.8 give a very different picture, and reveal a significant number of events of musical behaviour that underpin a diagnosis of autism, particularly the rigidity of the playing and the inability to engage in sharing and turn-taking in the playing, as evidenced by the number of events recorded under the category of resister. This example is taken from a previous article in *Music Therapy Perspectives* (Wigram 2000a)

9.3 Statistical analysis issues using the Improvisation Assessment Profiles

Finally, I would like to reflect on the potential for analysing numerical or categorical data from a functional analysis of musical improvisation. The functional, quantitative use I have made of the IAPs so far has involved scoring (counting) events in musical improvisation and assigning scores to predetermined categories (Wigram 1999b, 1999c, 2000a). For example, having decided that I want to look specifically at changes in tempo as a musical indicator related to autonomy, I have counted the number of times one or other person in a client – therapist improvisation changed tempo, and what provoked it. It is relatively easy to make a 'judgment' about the initiative that was taken to change tempo – whether it was independent or dependent on another, and to identify the event as standing somewhere on the gradients of the autonomy profile. This event, together with others within the same category (tempo, rhythmic ground) provides data that can be initially used for *descriptive statistics*. Descriptive statistics are essentially different from *inferential statistics*, and set out to summarize the experience. The difference can also be noted in drawing a distinction between samples and populations (Robson 1985; Rowntree 1991; West 1992). This is not so clear at first in Wheeler (1995), where Decuir initially suggests the use of descriptive statistics to identify parameters of a population or a sample. Inferential statistics, as Decuir later states clearly, allow the researcher to '...go beyond description to infer or estimate certain population characteristics based on a sample of the population.' Now the type of descriptive statistics that can be employed to quantify data analysis from the IAP's are clearly *measures of central tendency* (mean, mode, median and standard deviation), and to a lesser degree *correlation coefficients*.

Frequency data, such as numbers of events (as described above), is ripe for analysis through descriptive statistics, and appropriate conclusions can be drawn from such analysis in single cases. Neither the gradients in the IAPs, nor the scales can be scored using a *ratio* or *interval* scale, and therefore *parametric statistics* cannot be undertaken on a set of data if one is computing on the basis of equidistant points on a scale. However, *non-parametric* tests can be used. The value of non-parametric statistics is that rather than calculating the exact numerical difference between scores, and basing the statistical computation on this, non-parametric tests only take into account whether certain scores are higher or lower than other scores, effectively rank ordering the scores, as can be see in a Wilcoxon Signed-Ranks Test, Mann-Whitney U, a Friedman or a Kruskal-Wallis (Parametric equivalents: related t-test, unrelated t-test, 1-way ANOVA related or 1-way ANOVA unrelated respectively). Less robust, but applicable statistical tests are thus available should analysis comparing the number of scored events on an *ordinal* scale seem appropriate through rank ordering, and where the data is clearly not homogenous (Greene and D'Olivera 1989).

For a different type of analysis, categories can be developed and statistical tests applied (*chi-square*). The gradients on the IAPs could be treated as categories, and the assignment of musical elements defined as a whole series of sub-categories, i.e. *rhythmic ground follower, rhythmic ground leader, contrasting phrasing, rigid phrasing.* The normal use of the chi-square is where the data is *nominal* and the subjects are assigned to one or more categories. In the case of the IAPs the musical events could be assigned to categories, as in the example above. One is therefore attempting to find out whether there is some significant difference between categories. A chi-square can compute a comparison of the observed frequencies by which a number of events will fall into different categories (cells) with the expected frequencies for each 'category' if the differences are due to chance, as stated by the null hypothesis. It is important to note that a minimum number of at least twenty events (or subjects) is required to have enough allocated to each category (cell). The gradients on the IAPs are *ordinal* data, but can also be described as categories of description, response or interaction and therefore could lend themselves well to this type of statistical analysis.

IAPs are a highly sophisticated descriptive tool for undertaking qualitative analysis. Bruscia (1987) stated that they were used extensively as a teaching tool (p.410), and I would like to reinforce this aspect, because they are so useful in getting students to listen to what is happening, and then analyse it at a musical level, before jumping to conclusions in psychological, intuitive, but sometimes impetuous interpretation. Bruscia emphasizes the importance of listening to, and hearing what is happening in the improvised music, as he recommends the starting point for using the IAPs is with the salience profile. This profile helps identify which musical elements are most prominent, and exert most influence over other elements, and can be used to analyse intra-musical and inter-musical events. I think that when you know what you want to look for, you don't necessarily have to start with establishing the salience of musical elements – but if you are starting with a more 'open listening' approach, then the salience profile is the right starting point. There is, in my opinion, clearly a place for many different applications, methods of analysis and methods of interpretations using this IAP frame, and what is more important is that this model should be developed for a more systematic and widespread use internationally.

Conclusion

Musically structured or free improvisation provides a complex source of data for analysis, and the applied use of the Improvisation Assessment Profiles is effective in identifying music events that relate to therapeutic issues, as well as analysing creativity and musical interaction. Depending on the client(s), the analysis of musical material can provide concrete evidence in the form of the events that take place on specific musical elements to identify important aspects relating to the direction, process and outcome of therapy. It is necessary to make such an analysis in order to support and validate an intuitive understanding of a client's musical ability or creativity, without some of the significant and concrete events.

9.4 General conclusion

Improvisation gives us a very rich source of material for analysis. It seems unlikely that one would apply both the models of analysis described above to a given situation, yet it does depend on the question to be addressed: description or function of the music. The recommendations for the potential levels of analysis using the IAPs suggest they will answer both questions. However, the SMMA is a short, effective and inclusive way of describing all almost aspects of the music, without going on to undertake further, more detailed analysis.

   This brings me to the end of this book, closing a process that started, almost at a minimalist level, in Chapter 3 with a one-note improvisation here in Chapter 9 with a discussion about the complex analysis of multiple musical elements in improvisation. If this book can do one thing, I hope it leads people (musicians, therapists and clients) towards the sheer pleasure and enjoyment of improvising. Because it is a pleasure – and when I am teaching it, I spend more time trying to get students to relax, and listen with attention, heightened perception and expectation to the sounds they are making, and to love and nurture those sounds. We spend more of our lives being dissatisfied with what we do than satisfied. There is a valuable but sometimes destructive tendency to self-critique in humans that, when seen at its worst, results in the search for criticism even in the face of creativity, discovery and joy. To be able to feel proud and joyful when improvising, we must accept and perhaps ignore imperfection. Musicians who find improvisation most challenging are sometimes experienced and classically trained musicians, and it is perhaps because they are imprisoned by aspiring to the perfection of their 'ideal' musical selves – often driven by the influence of composers and performers significant to them. Break out of prison! Find your own music, create, explore, enjoy!

Bibliography

Alvin, J. (1975) *Music Therapy. Revised edition.* London: John Claire Books.

Bonde, L. O., Pedersen, N. I. and Wigram, T. (2001) *Nar ord ikke slaar til: En Haandbog i Musikterapiens Teori og Praksis i Danmark.* Aarhus: Klim.

Bruscia, K. (1987) *Improvisational Models of Music Therapy.* Springfield: Charles C. Thomas Publications.

Bruscia, K. (1994) 'Transference and counter-transference.' Unpublished lecture notes in Aalborg University, Department of Music Therapy.

Codding, P. (2000) 'Music Therapy Literature and Clinical Applications for Blind and Severely Visually Impaired Persons: 1940–2000.' In American Association of Music Therapy (2000) *Effectiveness of Music Therapy Procedures: Documentation of Research and Clinical Practice.* Silver Spring, Maryland: AMTA Inc. Publications.

Codding, P. (2002) 'A Comprehensive Survey of Music Therapists Practicing in Correctional Psychiatry: Demographics, Conditions of Employment, Service Provision, Assessment, Therapeutic Objectives and Related Values of the Therapist.' *Music Therapy Perspectives 20,* 56–69.

Collins Softback English Dictionary (1993) London: HarperCollins Publishers.

Di Franco, G. (1999) 'Music and Autism. Vocal Improvisation as Containment of Stereotypes.' In T. Wigram and J. De Backer (eds) *Music Therapy Applications in Developmental Disability, Paediatrics and Neurology.* London: Jessica Kingsley Publishers.

Edgerton, C. (1994) 'The Effect of Improvisational Music Therapy on the Communicative Behaviours of Autistic Children.' *Journal of Music Therapy 31,* 1, 31–62.

Erdonmez Grocke, D. E. (1999) 'A Phenomenological Study of Pivotal Moments in Guided Imagery and Music (GIM) Therapy.' University of Melbourne. *Dissertation Abstracts International* #9982778. Also published on CD-ROM III (2001) and CD-ROM IV (2002) University of Witten-Herdecke.

Grant, R. (1995) 'Music Therapy Assessment for Developmentally Disabled Adults.' In T. Wigram, B. Saperston and R. West (eds) *The Art and Science of Music Therapy: A Handbook.* London: Harwood Academic Publishers.

Greene, J. and D'Olivera, M. (1989) *Learning to Use Statistical Tests in Psychology.* Philadelphia: Open University Press.

Hevner, K. (1936) 'Experimental Studies of the Elements of Expression in Music.' *American Journal of Psychology 48,* 246–268.

Jarrett, K. (1997) 'How I Create.' *UNTE Reader,* July–August, 104.

Milano, D. (1984) 'Jazz Pianist and Psychiatrist Denny Zeitlin on the Psychology of Improvisation.' *Keyboard,* Oct. 25, 30–35.

Nettl, B. (1974) 'Thoughts on Improvisation – a Comparative Approach.' *Musical Quarterly,* January 1–19.

Nordoff, P. and Robbins, C. (1977) *Creative Music Therapy.* New York: Harper and Row Publishers.

Pavlicevic, M. (1995) 'Interpersonal Processes in Clinical Improvisation: Towards a Subjectively Objective Systematic Definition.' In T. Wigram, B. Saperston and R. West (eds) *The Art and Science of Music Therapy: a Handbook.* London: Harwood Academic Publishers.

Pavlicevic, M. (1997) *Music Therapy in Context: Music, Meaning and Relationship.* London: Jessica Kingsley Publishers.

Pedersen, I. N. (2002) 'Music Therapy with Psychiatric Clients.' In T. Wigram, I. Nygaard Pedersen and L. O. Bonde (eds) *A Comprehensive Guide to Music Therapy: Theory, Clinical Practice, Research and Training.* London: Jessica Kingsley Publishers.

Pressing, J. (1988) 'Improvisation: Methods and Models.' In J. A. Sloboda (ed) *Generative Processes in Music.* Oxford: Clarendon Press.

Priestley, M. (1975) *Music Therapy in Action.* London: Constable.

Priestley, M. (1994) *Essays on Analytical Music Therapy.* Gilsum, NH: Barcelona Publishers.

Raijmaekers, J. (1993) 'Music Therapy's Role in the Diagnosis of Psycho-geriatric Patients in the Hague.' In M. Heal and T. Wigram (eds) *Music Therapy in Health and Education.* London: Jessica Kingsley Publishers.

Robbins, C. and Robbins, C. (eds)(1998) *Healing Heritage: Paul Nordoff Exploring the Tonal Language of Music.* Gilsum, NH: Barcelona Publishers.

Robson, C. (1985) *Experiment, Design and Statistics in Psychology.* London: Pelican Books.

Rowntree, D. (1991) *Statistics without Tears.* London: Penguin Books.

Ruud, E. (1998) *Music Therapy: Improvisation, Communication and Culture.* Gilsum, NH: Barcelona Publishers.

Schwartz, D. (1998) 'The Search for Magic: Teaching Music Improvisation.' Unpublished master's thesis: University of East Anglia.

Sikström, M. and Skille, O. (1995) 'The Skille Musical Function Test as a Tool in the Assessment of Psychological Function and Individual Potential.' In T. Wigram, B. Saperston and R. West (eds) *The Art and Science of Music Therapy: A Handbook.* London: Harwood Academic Publishers.

Skewes, K. (2001) 'Examining the Experience of Group Music Therapy with Bereaved Adolescents: A Phenomenological Study.' PhD thesis, Melbourne University, Australia.

Staum, M. J. (2000) 'Music for Physical Rehabilitation: An Analysis of the Literature from 1950–1999 and Applications for Rehabilitation Settings.' In American Association of Music Therapy (2000) *Effectiveness of Music Therapy Procedures: Documentation of Research and Clinical Practice.* Silver Spring, Maryland: AMTA Inc. Publications.

West, R. (1992) *Computing for Psychologists. Statistical Analysis using SPSS and MINITAB.* London and Toronto: Harwood Academic Publishers.

Wheeler, B. (ed) (1995) *Music Therapy Research: Quantitive and Qualitative Perspectives.* Phoenixville, Philadelphia: Barcelona Publishers.

Wigram T. (1995a) 'Improvisazione tematica: Transfert e controtransfert positivo e negativo.' In G. Di Franco and R. de Michele (eds) *Musicoterapia in Italia: Scuola handicap salute mentale.* Naples: Casa Editrice Idelsen. (Thematic Improvisation: Positive and Negative Transference and Counter-transference in the Music Therapy Process. Paper for the Italian National Congress of Music Therapy, 1994, Naples.)

Wigram, T. (1995b) 'Musicoterapia: Estructura y flexibilidad en el proceso de musicoterapia.' In P. del Campo (ed) *La musica como proceso humano.* Salamanca: Amaru Ediciones.

Wigram, T. (1996a) '"Becoming Clients": Role Playing Clients as a Technique in the Training of Advanced Level Music Therapy Students.' Paper to the 3rd European Music Therapy Conference, Aalborg, Denmark. In L. O. Bonde and I. N. Pedersen (eds) *Music Therapy Within Multi-Disciplinary Teams.* Aalborg: Aalborg University Press.

Wigram, T. (1996b) 'From Theory to Practice: Role Playing Clients as an Experiential Technique to Develop Music Therapy Skills with Advanced Level Music Therapy Students.' Paper to the 8th World Conference of Music Therapy, Hamburg, 1996 (awaiting publication).

Wigram T. (1996c) 'The Effect of Vibroacoustic Therapy on Clinical and Non-Clinical Populations.' PhD thesis, St George's Medical School, University of London. In D. Aldridge and J. Fachner (eds) *Info CD-ROM IV*. Herdecke: University of Witten Herdecke.

Wigram, T. (1999a) 'Lectures and Workshops in Developing Clinical Piano Improvisation Skills.' Music Therapy Department, Aalborg University. Unpublished communication.

Wigram, T. (1999b) 'Assessment Methods in Music Therapy: A Humanistic or Natural Science Framework?' *Nordisk Tidsskrift for Musikterapi 8*, 1, 6–24.

Wigram, T. (1999c) 'Variability and Autonomy in Music Therapy Interaction: Evidence for the Diagnosis and Therapeutic Intervention for Children with Autism and Asperger Syndrome.' In R. Pratt and D. Erdonmez Grocke (eds) *MusicMedicine 3: MusicMedicine and Music Therapy: Expanding Horizons*. Melbourne: Faculty of Music, University of Melbourne.

Wigram, T. (2000a) 'A Method of Music Therapy Assessment for the Diagnosis of Autistic and Communication Disordered Children.' *Music Therapy Perspectivess 18*, 1.

Wigram, T. (2000b) 'Lectures and Workshops in Developing Clinical Piano Improvisation Skills.' Music Therapy Department, Aalborg University. Unpublished communication.

Wigram, T. (2001) 'Lectures and Workshops to the Efetruddalses 2 aar undervising for Cand. Mag i Musikterapi. Developing Clinical Piano Improvisation Skills.' Music Therapy Department, Aalborg University. Unpublished communication.

Wigram, T. (2002a) 'Indications in Music Therapy: Evidence from Assessment that can identify the Expectations of Music Therapy as a Treatment for Autistic Spectrum Disorder (ASD): Meeting the Challenge of Evidence Based Practice.' *British Journal of Music Therapy 16*, 1.

Wigram, T. (2002b) 'Physiological Reponses to Music.' In T. Wigram, I. Nygaard Pedersen and L. O. Bonde (eds) *A Comprehensive Guide to Music Therapy: Theory, Clinical Practice, Research and Training*. London: Jessica Kingsley Publishers.

Wigram, T. and De Backer, J. (1999a) *Clinical Applications of Music Therapy in Developmental Disability, Paediatrics and Neurology*. London: Jessica Kingsley Publishers.

Wigram, T. and De Backer, J. (1999b) *Clinical Applications of Music Therapy in Psychiatry*. London: Jessica Kingsley Publishers.

Wigram, T. and Bonde, L. O. (2002) 'Musical Skills in Music Therapy.' In T. Wigram, I. Nygaard Pedersen and L. O. Bonde (eds) *A Comprehensive Guide to Music Therapy: Theory, Clinical Practice, Research and Training*. London: Jessica Kingsley Publishers.

Wigram, T., De Backer, J. and Van Camp, J. (1999) 'Music Therapy Training: A process to develop the musical and therapeutic identity of the music therapist.' In T. Wigram and J. De Backer (eds) *Clinical Applications of Music Therapy in Developmental Disablity, Paediatrics and Neurology*. London: Jessica Kingsley Publishers.

Wigram, T. and Dileo, C. (1997) *Music, Vibration and Health*. Pipersville, PA: Jeffrey Books.

Wigram, T., Nygaard Pedersen, I. and Bonde, L.O. (2002) *A Comprehensive Guide to Music Therapy: Theory, Clinical Practice, Research and Training*. London: Jessica Kingsley Publishers.

Subject Index

Author Index